JANDAMARRA AND THE BUNUBA RESISTANCE

Dear Ro

thank you for visiting us in Westen Australia.

this is very good pre-reading for your next visit.... to the Kimberley !!)

We can't wait to go there with you.... it'll simultaneously blow your mind & take your breath away

love love love

NRCZ

xxxx

Banjo Woorunmurra, Bunuba Elder, kept the story alive
through his custodianship. He passed away in 2003.

A true Australian hero
Paul Kelly

JANDAMARRA AND THE BUNUBA RESISTANCE

BANJO WOORUNMURRA & HOWARD PEDERSEN

Magabala Books

FOREWORD

AS A YOUNG GIRL GROWING up in Bunuba country I heard Jandamarra's story from my old people many times. While the story was known by all Bunuba people, Grandfather Wirranmarra (Banjo Woorunmurra) knew the full version. It was his responsibility to keep telling the story so that we, the Bunuba people, would never lose our history, our sense of wonder at the magic and power of our country and the knowledge of the deep injustices inflicted on our people from those who invaded our country.

Grandfather Wirranmarra took his responsibility seriously. He not only kept the Jandamarra story alive in the Bunuba oral tradition but he made sure the story became widely known. *Jandamarra and the Bunuba Resistance*, first published in 1995 by Magabala Books, is a vital part of taking Jandamarra's story to a wider audience. The book was a remarkable collaboration between Grandfather Wirranmarra and historian Howard Pedersen – but telling Jandamarra's story has been a Bunuba community endeavour.

The Bunuba community commissioned the writing of the book and many of us participated in its production as guides on country, storytellers and editors. As a community we retraced our people's history and, by combining our oral tradition with information from the written records, we have been able to piece together the story that we, the Bunuba people, own.

Writing the book and working towards making a feature film on Jandamarra has been an empowering process for our community. Bunuba people own Leopold Downs and Fairfield stations and run successful cattle operations on lands that are central to the Jandamarra story. We celebrate our law and culture on these lands as our ancestors did for thousands of years. Our song men and women sing and dance the Yilimbirri junba (corroborree), the legend of Jandamarra.

The Jandamarra play was showcased at the 2008 Perth International Arts Festival to packed audiences and toured the Kimberley in 2011. Jandamarra has generated illustrated children's books, a documentary film by Mitch Torres and songs by artists like Paul Kelly, Ted Egan and Mark Bin Bakar.

Jandamarra and the Bunuba Resistance has been reprinted several times and will keep selling because the story, like the man, will never fade away. Jandamarra is a hero of the Bunuba people as well as to people from many other Aboriginal nations. He stands as a unifying figure – a champion of justice who can be admired by all Australians.

Jandamarra's story is making its mark on the nation's heritage. This would not have been possible without Grandfather Wirranmarra's unyielding commitment to telling the story to the world. As his partnership with Howard Pedersen demonstrated, he was a staunch advocate for collaboration and reconciliation, which he saw as the living spirit of Jandamarra.

Nyanyjili Thalbagbiya June Oscar
Bunuba leader

BUNUBA PLACE NAMES

Balili – limestone, Napier Range
Bandaral ngarri – Fitzroy River
Bandilngan – Windjana Gorge
Baraa – Tunnel Creek
Danggu – Geikie Gorge
Galanganyja – black soil plains
Ganimbiri – Oscar Range
Guinyja – Brooking Gorge
Gunbi – Mt Broome
Gurangadja – Brooking Springs
Limalurru – Lillimooloora
Mayalnga – Margaret River
Milawundi – King Leopold Range

CONTENTS

PREFACE

THIS BOOK COULD NOT HAVE been written without the knowledge, inspiration and guidance of Banjo Woorunmurra. Born in 1915 at Fairfield Station in the West Kimberley, Banjo was the senior custodian of the Jandamarra story and a living repository of much of his people's history. His traditional Bunuba land takes in country where Jandamarra and other Bunuba people fought heroically to defend their homelands against white invasion in the late nineteenth century.

I first met Banjo in 1977 at Fitzroy Crossing. I was then twenty-two and ill-prepared for what I encountered in that dusty little town. My life until then had been comfortable, complacent and fairly predictable. Aboriginal Australia had hardly touched my consciousness.

Many people I knew travelled to Britain and Europe in their early twenties. I hitch-hiked around Australia in search of a country I felt I belonged to. In Fitzroy Crossing I learnt more about this nation than I could ever have hoped to understand from the comfort of urban Australia. Here Aboriginal people were the overwhelming majority of the population. At the time, Fitzroy Crossing's population was about two thousand. Only a handful were non-Aboriginal and they were mostly in jobs that serviced the local community. Hardly anybody appeared to live in a house. Shelters made of sheets of corrugated iron and canvas dotted the landscape. The Crossing Inn seemed to be the town's commercial and social centre, where people fuelled cars, bought food and drank. And police seemed to be everywhere, putting people in the back of paddy wagons and taking them to the lockup.

Banjo made the whole scene comprehensible to me. He described how most people had come to Fitzroy only recently, after they were no longer wanted on the pastoral stations, following the equal wage decision in the late 1960s. This was Bunuba country, he explained, but the Bunuba were relatively small in number compared with the dispossessed Walmajarri, Wangkajunga, Gooniyandi, Nyikina and Mangala people, who flooded into Fitzroy Crossing in the late 1960s and early 1970s. He told me of the injustices suffered by local people at the hands of the police, and the pastoralists who denied the traditional owners access to their lands.

Like so many Aboriginal people, Banjo Woorunmurra tells stories with a sense of poetry that connects the past to the living present. His stories of how some of his parents' generation were shot or poisoned and the survivors enslaved by the early colonisers challenged the foundation of my understanding of Australian history. 'Did your people fight back?' I asked innocently. He then told me the story of Jandamarra.

Banjo's stories inspired me to study history at Perth's Murdoch University. There I read Ion Idriess' novel on Jandamarra, *Outlaws of the Leopolds*, published in 1952. It is an engaging account but, as the title suggests, the central character is depicted as a criminal who defied the legitimate laws of white society. I read the same police files on which Idriess based his book but interpreted these primary sources somewhat differently. Idriess did not mention the massacres by police and settlers that Banjo and other Aboriginal people had described to me in detail. Nor did Idriess place the story in the context of an invasion, with Jandamarra and other Aboriginal people defending their lands and religion against a brutal assault.

I wrote an honours thesis on the subject in 1980 and a few years later had an article on Jandamarra published in a Western Australian historical journal, but still I couldn't let the story go. In many visits to the Kimberley, I stayed in contact with Banjo and conversed with many Aboriginal people who spoke about their lives and recalled the memories of past generations. In 1985, Banjo suggested that I write a book on Jandamarra based on his and other Bunuba people's oral histories, fused with police, newspaper and other written historical sources.

It was an exciting prospect but it proved more difficult than I had ever imagined. With assistance from the Australian Bicentennial Authority I was able to take time off work to research and write. I spent several weeks in the Fitzroy Crossing area talking to Bunuba people, and months in the State Library reading everything I could find that shed light on the story. I quickly realised that a white historian could not reflect the essence of the Bunuba stories. Jandamarra was magic – a supernatural being who could not be destroyed by police or settler bullets. He could only be challenged by an Aboriginal man who also possessed such powers. Much of the Bunuba story is about the spiritual significance of land and the law that flows from it.

The integration of these stories into a western historical narrative is highly problematic. Much of the information is secret and cannot be written for public consumption. Also, Aboriginal perceptions of the past and explanations about why certain events occurred do not sit easily within western historical chronology and our understandings of cause and effect.

This book does not pretend to be written from an Aboriginal perspective. That task awaits the creativity and insight of Aboriginal writers. However, the Bunuba oral testimonies were fundamentally important to a story that draws primarily on information contained within reports, diaries and journals written by the invaders. These written sources can not be and have not been taken at face value. Interpreting them as sources of historical explanation would have been impossible without the Bunuba oral history.

Howard Pedersen

INTRODUCTION

IN THE STILLNESS OF A hot October night in 1894, the sound of a single rifle shot echoed against the nearby cliff-face. With his smoking Winchester rifle, Jandamarra stood over the corpse of a policeman. Nearby, a group of prisoners who were chained to a tree awaited their liberation.

Bill Richardson had been a policeman for just six months. He was highly rated, measured by the large numbers of Aboriginal people he had captured. His success was due almost entirely to the extraordinary talents of Jandamarra, who rode with him on patrol.

This had been a remarkably successful patrol. Sixteen prisoners were being chain-marched to prison less than 100 miles from where the Bunuba – the owners of the central Kimberley highlands – had resisted white incursion into their country for almost a decade.

The prisoners were senior men of the Bunuba people and without them the Bunuba defences were unquestionably shattered. A short distance away, 500 cattle were slowly being herded along the dry sandy river bed to pasture beyond the Kimberley ranges, a fortress protecting the Bunuba lands. Extremely fertile, this country, prior to white invasion, supported up to two thousand people.

The fate of thousands of years of Bunuba tradition and culture lay in the hands of Jandamarra. This was his country and the men on the policeman's chain were his family. Caught up in the complex web of first contact with white colonisation, this young man was confused, trapped in a tragic dilemma, his own personal survival against powerful obligations to his people and the awesome spiritual law that enriched his country.

Undisciplined sexual encounters with women had led his people's lawmen to banish Jandamarra to another world. He sought refuge in a community of strangers: weird people with no sense of belonging to a land they fought ruthlessly to possess.

The white people, whom the Bunuba called Malngarri, embraced Jandamarra from a young age. They taught him their language, stockwork, horsemanship and – the pinnacle of all frontier skills – the mastery of the gun. He soon learnt to fire the rifle with greater precision than any white person he knew.

Jandamarra was much more than a useful frontier servant. To the small West Kimberley settler community, he symbolised their own fragile moral superiority over a people who greatly outnumbered them and who remained in possession of the fertile, rolling hills and the formidable mountains of yet unconquered lands. This young man had seemingly rejected his own people to embrace the new and advancing order.

The blast of gunfire on that fateful night, followed by more shootings days later when the liberated Bunuba prisoners attacked the stockmen who were herding the cattle, shattered the confidence of the settlers. Jandamarra brought to his people an ability to fight the settlers on their terms. Assuming the status of military commander, he made the gun his mark of leadership. Marshalling his followers, this renowned marksman hastily assembled a Bunuba fighting force, armed it with stolen weaponry and engaged the enemy in battle.

In the previous ten years of skirmishes with police and settlers, Bunuba raiders had prevented the squatters from occupying their hill country. Hit-and-run attacks on both sheep and stockmen's huts became the hallmark of Bunuba resistance in a sustained guerilla war. The gun, the symbol of white frontier supremacy, was suddenly in the hands of Aboriginal warriors. Momentarily, the ascendancy was won by the Bunuba.

Jandamarra was a genius who excelled in both the world to which he belonged and the world that had adopted him. But he could never have predicted the capacity of his enemy to inflict overwhelming military terror. The scattered settler community mobilised, and with reinforcement police troopers from outside the district, launched a murderous campaign sanctioned by political authority in faraway Perth. This was terror on a relentless scale, designed to crush Aboriginal people into permanent subjection.

This bloody history can be told because it is etched powerfully in the collective memories of today's Kimberley Aboriginal people. Yet white written history does not record the extent of killing during the Kimberley's early colonisation. Official records under-state the bloodshed. Police journals and settlers' diaries gloss over the genocidal violence, the slaughter of Aboriginal men, women and children. There is no mention of the distribution of food laced with poison so that Aboriginal people would suffer agonising deaths in the bush. Concealed at the time and hidden from white historical accounts ever since, this was a war never acknowledged by Western Australian society.

Over the corpses of his compatriots, Jandamarra transcended the physical horrors of war. He was seen to be blessed with qualities owned by spiritually empowered people. To the Bunuba his great legend is the power of his magic. A mabarn man or Jalnggangurru, as the Bunuba called him, he could defy police bullets and disappear like a ghost. Casting aside European strategies of violence he used these powers to taunt and ridicule settlers and police for over two years. In an amazing campaign of non-violent resistance, Jandamarra single-handedly blocked the settlers' path to some of the richest grazing lands in Western Australia.

The chapters that follow tell the story of the most remarkable struggle against colonial occupation in Western Australian history. Ironically, the lands envisaged by those first Englishmen as the home for a new and humane world became stained with the blood of its original inhabitants.

COLONISATION

IN 1837 BRITISH EYES GAZED at the map of the world and focused on a region of north-western Australia to cradle yet another colonising experiment. Even though this region's coastline had been surveyed by foreigners, the interior was known only to the people who had lived on these lands for thousands of generations.

This region was mostly fertile, with heavy life-bringing rains that deluged the lands in the summer months. Permanent water above and below the ground produced an abundant food supply that was readily hunted and gathered. Few regions of Aboriginal Australia were as densely populated as this. In 1932, the eminent anthropologist AP Elkin estimated that the region sustained a permanent population of ten thousand people before the invasion. But Elkin had not properly accounted for the thousands who were slaughtered by the armed invaders or who had died as a result of introduced diseases such as smallpox, measles, influenza and leprosy. The real figure may have been as high as thirty thousand.

The Indigenous people of this vast area were not a homogenous cultural group. There were nearly fifty different language groups, which were in turn divided into various dialects. Smaller bands, based on extended families, had clear land and sea-owning responsibilities.

Thousands of people lived near the coast and would suffer the full force of the British invasion. These people's ownership responsibility for their country extended way beyond the blue water horizon. To the south of this vast region, where fertile grassy plains merged into desert, lived the Karajarri. The Karajarri were to be devastated by pearlers who pillaged their traditional country for oysters and enslaved the traditional owners for use as pearl divers and sex chattels. After pearlers had stripped the mudflats of pearl shell the government established a telegraph station, then a ration camp at La Grange Bay, named by the French. The surviving Karajarri were joined much later by the Mangala, Nyangumarta and other desert groups living under oppressively paternalistic church rule.

The pearlers moved a little to the north and centred their industry around a place the British had named Roebuck Bay. Here the Yawuru, Jugun and Ngumbarl feared a similar fate to that of the Karajarri. Further to the north, on a large peninsula named after the navigator, naturalist and adventurer William Dampier, lived the Nimanburru, Jabirrjabirr, Nyulnyul and Bardi. These people would also suffer horrifically at the hands of the pearlers, the survivors often being forcibly removed onto Catholic and Protestant missions established at places called Beagle Bay, Lombadina and Sunday Island.

Where the coastline eats into the land mass, creating a huge expanse of shallow muddy water that the British named King Sound, lived the Warrwa. At the southernmost point of the sound, near the mouth of the region's mightiest river, the invaders established their first permanent colonial outpost and named it Derby. Such was the brutal impact of this first colonial settlement that only a handful of Warrwa survived into the twentieth century.

Further along the northern coast and out into the blue ocean, which was punctuated by thousands of small islands, lived the

Jawi, Yawijibaya and Winjarumi. These societies were demolished by the rampaging seafarers who captured men and women to work on the pearl boats. Many of those who remained were forcibly taken to the church missions on the mainland.

The north-western and most northerly parts of this vast Kimberley region were owned by the Unggarrangu, Umiida, Worrorra, Wunambal, Gaambera, Wila Wila, Miwa, Kwini, Munumburru and Yiiji. These people had experienced contact for hundreds of years with Asian fishing people, from northern islands that now belong to the Indonesian archipelago, and were some of the first people to confront the inquisitive explorers from Britain. Ironically they were to suffer least from the invasion in the early years as their country was deemed economically unsuitable for British occupation.

Many years after the beginning of white occupation, these more northerly people suffered the horrors of the cruel contagious leprosy disease, which spread through their communities. Grief stricken and disoriented, most lepers were herded onto the mission compounds of Pago Pago, Kulumburu, Kunmunya, Watjalum and Forrest River, where agents of the Catholic, Presbyterian and Anglican churches, with a few exceptions, imposed practices designed to destroy their languages, religion and cultural traditions. Those who were forcibly transported to the Government concentration camp-like settlement at Munja, near the banks of the picturesque Walcott Inlet, fared little better.

The stroke of an imperial pen drawn on a map by people in the Colonial Office in faraway London defined the region's eastern border. The lands on the other side became the Northern Territory and were successively governed by people in London, Adelaide, Canberra and Darwin.

Along this eastern border and stretching westward lay fertile mountainous country. The explorers, who foreshadowed the invasion of the pastoralists and their cattle, named the rivers that cut through the red sandstone mountains; introduced stock in their thousands would soon pasture along the grassy valleys. The rivers included the Ord, Pentecost, Durack, King, Turner and Panton. The traditional owners of this country were the Doolboong, Gajirrawoong, Miriwoong, Kija, Malngin and Ngarnawu.

No church missions were established in this country because the cattlemen who occupied it desperately needed the people they had dispossessed to manage and muster the cattle herds. The mountainous terrain, however, allowed traditional owners to fight the invaders for a number of decades. In the first decade of the twentieth century Aboriginal families remained independent, and from high in the mountains looked down on pastoral settlements. The guerilla warfare subsided between 1910 and 1920, when the government created Violet Valley and Moola Bulla reserves, supposedly for Aboriginal benefit: moves that were seen by the traditional owners as a gesture of peace. Yet massacres by police and settlers continued in the area until at least 1926.

To the south of this fertile and spectacular mountainous country lay the rocky, hilly and spinifex-grass plains country of the Jaru. The Jaru were to suffer the full brunt of a short-lived gold rush in the 1880s, which saw thousands of diggers pour into the region to scour the creek beds and washaways in search of the precious metal. A small settlement to service the gold diggers was established and named Halls Creek. These diggers were violent men who met any resistance from the Jaru with bloodthirsty retaliation.

This was arid country but it didn't stop the cattlemen pushing the frontier forever southward until a lack of water and a sea of desert sands stopped them. The southern desert expanses of this huge region of northern Western Australia are owned by the Kukatja, Wangkajunga, Walmajarri and Mangala. Their lands have never been occupied or their traditional land title extinguished by subsequent actions of governments.

Not far north of the Walmajarri desert lands is a formidable mountain range that divides the region. The Aboriginal people called this range Milawundi. Alexander Forrest, the first explorer to survey this area in advance of colonial conquest, tried to cut through Milawundi and failed. To Forrest these mountains evoked within him a sense of imperial awe. He named Milawundi the King Leopold Range after the Belgian monarch who had recently carved out a huge colonial empire in the African continent on behalf of his minuscule European nation.

These mountains draw huge tropical rains, creating a mosaic of waterways. Here the region's mightiest river is sourced. The Fitzroy River or Bandaral ngarri, named after a British coastal surveyor, snakes westward to its mouth on the tidal mudflats of King Sound. The Bandaral ngarri pours more water from its mouth than the combined volume of a score of other major Australian rivers.

The country where the Bandaral ngarri begins belongs to the Bunuba. This is extremely fertile land and before the invasion was the most densely populated in the whole region. The Bunuba enjoyed a quality of life that would have been the envy of most people on earth. Their rivers and creeks were laden with fish and freshwater crocodiles. Over the lands moved a large variety of animal life such as kangaroos, rock wallabies, bush turkeys, goannas, emus, snakes, lizards and bats. Fruit and vegetables grew all year round but flourished particularly during the monsoonal wet season. Land and water animals were not hunted indiscriminately, nor were fruit and vegetables gathered at random. Hunting was governed by religious and kinship principles that bound the people to the land and made sure that the food supply was guaranteed forever.

North of the Bunuba lands lay the expansive country of the Ngarinyin people. To the east lived the Worla and Gooniyandi. South of the Bandaral ng̲arri lived the Walmajarri. Beyond the Bunuba western boundary were the lands of the Nyikina and Unggumi.

This whole region was incorporated into the British Empire in 1829, when Captain James Stirling planted the Union Jack on the banks of the Swan River, over two thousand miles to the south. Fifty years later the colony's northernmost region was named the Kimberley after the British Secretary of State for the Colonies.

The Kimberley, whose land mass is greater than that of the entire United Kingdom, was the last non-desert region of the Australian continent to be colonised. In 1837, when the first British explorers landed on the Kimberley's shores to assess the region for future colonial settlement, Sydney had already been established for nearly fifty years. British settlements that later became State capitals were established across the continent and named Hobart, Perth, Melbourne, Brisbane and Adelaide. Land-hungry sheep graziers, known as squatters, were pushing relentlessly inland from these coastal settlements and destroying Aboriginal societies in the process of taking their land.

In 1833, Britain became the first nation in Europe to formally ban the practice of slavery from its expansive empire. The humanitarian lobby, which had been instrumental in making slavery illegal under British law, was also influential in the 1835 House of Commons report into Australian settlement. That report said in part that Aboriginal people 'of any land have an incontrovertible right to their own soil: a plain and sacred right, however, which seems not to have been understood. Europeans have entered their borders, uninvited, and when there, have not only acted as if they were undoubted lords of the soil, but have punished the natives as aggressors if they have evinced a disposition to live in their own country'.[1]

George Grey, the instigator and leader of the British Kimberley exploration party in December 1837, was associated with the British humanitarian society. A young idealistic British army officer, Grey was posted to Ireland after he graduated from Sandhurst military college. He soon detested his military duties, particularly the extracting of taxes from Irish peasants to fund the British-imposed Church of Ireland, and came to secretly sympathise with the Irish nationalist cause. He returned to London a disillusioned man and became convinced that the misery of poverty and class conflict had taken a firm grip on British society. Engulfed by a feeling he described as 'a nightmare of darkness', Grey looked to the lands of north-west Australia to give 'mankind a new start'.[2]

Landing at a place the British named Hanover Bay in Worrorra country on the north-western Kimberley coast, Grey and his party explored the coastal region around the Glenelg and Prince Regent rivers. Describing the country as 'rich as any other spots upon the globe', the romantic was convinced that here was the paradise where the British could build a new world. His vision was to create a new society where British immigrants would live in harmony with Aboriginal people.

Part of Grey's instructions from the British Government was 'to familiarise the natives with the British name and character'.[3] Grey's party intruded arrogantly into sacred places to copy down on notepaper the paintings that adorned cave walls. From hastily deserted Worrorra campsites, Grey and his men stole ceremonial objects to take back to London. Finally, after several weeks without any courteous interaction with Worrorra people, Grey and his men found themselves surrounded by a large group of men who angrily gestured to the intruders to leave their country. Grey stood his ground, only to be greeted by a flurry of spears. One struck him and before collapsing through loss of blood, he opened fire with his musket, shooting a man in the back, then watched him die in the arms of his distressed countrymen.

Despite the British Government's support of Grey's 1837 exploration it did not respond to Grey's exceedingly positive report recommending the establishment of a British colonial settlement in the Kimberley. The British were too concerned about the survival of the small colonial outpost at Swan River in the south to plan another expansionary adventure in the tropical north.

Perth was established as the administrative capital of the Swan River colony in 1829. The settlers could barely feed themselves. Within a few years attacks on the settlers by the traditional owners, the Noongars, almost caused the British to withdraw from Australia's western coast. Instead, 200 or more Nyoongar men, women and children were massacred at Pinjarra, south of Perth, in 1834. The toll was officially understated at less than thirty. Following this so-called 'battle', the frontier encroached slowly over the dry sandy lands, and sheep grazing was introduced. But Aboriginal attacks continued against the settlers, who were too small in number to secure the lands and create an economy that could sustain them. By the late 1840s the colony that became known as Western Australia began losing its settlers as people migrated to safer and more prosperous settlements in eastern Australia.

In an attempt to inject life into its dying economy, convicts from England and Ireland were transported to Western Australia. For the next eighteen years, ten thousand convicts were shipped to Western Australia to work on farms and public infrastructure but this was not enough to stimulate growth for the fledgling colony's economy.

While eastern Australia experienced a huge influx of settler population, lured mainly by gold, the white population in the west remained virtually stagnant, only the convicts providing any real population increase. Perth colonists looked to the far north in the hope that it could generate the spark to ignite the dormant Western Australian economy.

In the early 1860s, Grey's exploration journals were re-read, prompting intrepid men to mount expeditions to assess the north's economic potential. Grey's observations were confirmed and the rush to colonise the north began.

Most of the interest came from the land-hungry squattocracy of western Victoria. Proposing to lease four million acres from the Western Australian Government in the area Grey had explored, two hundred Victorians banded together to form the Camden Harbour Association. Grazing sheep among an abundance of tropical fruit and cotton was the romantic scenario painted by the scheme's promoters. These men, who purported to fulfil Grey's vision, predicted the new lands would give rise to the creation of a great city rivalling Singapore.

The excitement was contagious and within months Victoria's Western District gave birth to another enterprising scheme, the Denison Plains Association. This company sought to stock land in arid country bordering the Great Sandy Desert, in the south-eastern Kimberley.

Fearing the Victorians would form an independent colony in the Kimberley, Western Australia decided to stamp its political authority on the northern lands. In August 1864 an expedition funded by the Western Australian Government sailed from Fremantle to explore the Kimberley coastal country between Camden Harbour and Roebuck Bay. Frederick Panter, the expedition's leader, reported that the land around Roebuck Bay was equal 'to the best runs in Victoria' and estimated that it could graze over one million sheep.

Within weeks, the colony's leading squatters and merchants formed the Roebuck Bay Association. Modelled along the lines of the two Victorian colonising associations, it was the first organised Western Australian attempt to colonise the north. The Association's advance party sailed from Fremantle in October 1864, farewelled by cheering crowds and a gunfire salute; the whole colony was infected with enthusiasm. 'The days of our dependence on the parent state are numbered,'[4] claimed a Perth newspaper.

Late in 1864, ships sailed from Fremantle, Melbourne and Portland harbours to the far north of Western Australia to begin a colonisation which, many hoped, would awaken Western Australia from its economic slumber. Yet the enthusiastic push to colonise the north ended in failure.

Members of the Denison Plains Association did not even reach the Kimberley shores to begin their overland passage. The Camden Harbour experiment also collapsed. Within a year of its establishment in December 1864, all surviving settlers abandoned the place. Many others had died from sunstroke and fever. Their legacy was a few scattered buildings and the bodies of several Worrorra, who were slaughtered in the invaders' futile efforts to secure their lands.

The Roebuck Bay settlement collapsed also. These prospective sheep-graziers established themselves on land that was of immense cultural significance to the Yawuru. They were joined by some remnants of the Camden Harbour fiasco who were determined not to retreat a second time from these northern shores. Under constant attack by the Yawuru, who made it clear that the invaders should leave their sacred grounds, the leaders of the Association decided to explore the country south of Roebuck Bay in search of more land to graze their sheep. The party of three, Panter, Harding and policeman Goldwyer, soon met their deaths at the hands of Karajarri warriors near an area that would later be occupied by the La Grange telegraph station. The Roebuck Bay Association abruptly abandoned the place in late 1865, but not before a small but heavily armed party sent from Perth had scoured the area, killing a number of Aboriginal people in revenge.

By the late 1860s, north-western colonisation amounted to a few scattered sheep stations occupied mostly by the remnants of the three failed associations, in a region that later became known as the Pilbara. Here, squatters suffering high transport costs, low wool prices and severe labour shortages held the lands tenuously. Their economic salvation was the discovery of pearl shells in abundance along the coast. Northern Western Australia would soon become the world's largest supplier of pearlshell to British clothing manufacturers clamouring for the product to make buttons. Almost every north-west pastoralist formed an economic relationship with seafaring pearl masters to share the profits.

Initially, the pearling industry depended almost entirely on the enslavement of Aboriginal divers. Despite the fact that many came from inland regions, their ability to dive deep and remain underwater for a long time was highly prized by the pearlers. Aboriginal communities were torn apart as countless young men and women were taken from their homelands and forced onto ships scattered along the coast. The capture of large numbers of Aboriginal divers, many of whom suffered lonely and horrific deaths, was made possible through the close collaboration between pearlers and the sheep graziers. Both groups made significant profits from a system of slavery that supported European occupation of the north. By the end of the 1870s, northern colonisation accounted for fewer than 300 white settlers, whose economic survival depended on the work of over one thousand Aboriginal people on sheep stations and pearling boats.

The much-lauded northern vision, which promised to deliver an influx of settlers and wealth to the colony, had failed. While all other Australian colonies had become politically independent, the fewer than thirty thousand Western Australian settlers suffered economic stagnation with little prospect of freeing themselves from British political control.

The only answer to the colony's woes, it seemed, was to find more fertile land for sheep. In 1878, the government sent two of the colony's favourite sons to explore the upper reaches of the north-western rivers in search of new pastures. The brothers John and Alexander

Forrest returned to Perth with the depressing news that, as the Pilbara rivers were traced eastward, they dried up in desert sands. The only possibility of pastoral expansion, they reported, was to the north, where pearl slavers had observed fertile grassy plains along the mighty Bandaral ngarri.

The following year, Alexander Forrest led the first white men to venture far into the Kimberley hinterland. Here were lands rich and diverse. Spectacular mountain ranges cast shadows over fertile river valleys, and savannah plains dotted with waterholes stretched to desert sand horizons. A land of power and beauty supported animal and plant life in abundance. This was a land irresistibly attractive to European economic interests.

Alexander Forrest's report did not dwell on the fact that the Yawuru and Karajarri had defeated earlier white attempts to colonise this region. Instead, he wrote positively of the large numbers of Aboriginal people he saw and claimed that they would be useful servants for the settlers, who would come in droves to occupy the region. He didn't appreciate the diversity of language and culture of the thousands of traditional owners who lived there. Each of these language groups was like a separate nation, although the concept of nation-state did not exist in the Aboriginal world. Group identity was determined by common language, kinship relations and a spiritual, ancestral connection with land.

The explorers and the settlers who followed refused to acknowledge or could not comprehend the depth of religious significance that linked Aboriginal people to their land. Concepts of private tenure were non-existent. Aboriginal people belonged to the land as much as the land belonged to the people. This was a world where the physical and spiritual meshed as one and where the earth was not cultivated nor animals husbanded on it. Land for Aboriginal people supplied food and resources for shelter, hunting equipment and various tools.

But the religious significance was all-consuming. People, land, animals and the ancestral life were bound together in a spiritual web. In this world, enriched and sustained by ceremonial business, land title-deeds were not transferable pieces of paper but immutable sacred songs, boards and rites.

These beliefs were not to be threatened by outsiders. Land was irrefutably sacred. If it were not respected or properly protected, mysterious and violent forces could cause great harm. Only custodians of the secret law and their families could feel part of this land and therefore live on it, manage it and enrich it, not only for themselves and their ancestors but for the generations who would follow. The land's guardians could only be those who knew the secret stories of its creation by those omnipotent Dreamtime heroes.

Marriage, religious ceremonies, hunting and gathering or simply socialising allowed people access to foreign country. But they were visitors whose social and moral authority was weakened when they were separated from their own lands. Even illegitimate intruders from a neighbouring clan or language group, who occasionally raided to kidnap people or target somebody for vengeance, would strike quickly and then retreat to their own country.

Before colonisation, Aboriginal society was void of military tradition. Battles between opposing groups were normally well-orchestrated cultural events and not prompted by disputes over land ownership. An army was not needed because the group did not plan invasions or feel threatened by invaders; furthermore, who would command such an army?

This was a society whose leaders had authority on the basis of religious and cultural status. An individual's authority came from accumulated knowledge of the law of the land. These were the lawmen – the high priests of Aboriginal society. They did not make laws, they inherited them from a living spiritual force. It was their responsibility to teach others and make sure that the knowledge of the law was passed to the next generation.

These hunters and gatherers rarely assembled in large numbers and when they did it was usually for law or ceremonies. The family group was the fundamental component of the society. Small bands travelled well-trodden paths on clearly demarcated lands. Sound land management ensured food supply for present and successive generations. Here was a people in remarkable coexistence with the physical environment, guided overwhelmingly by religious values.

Forrest understood nothing of the society he visited. Returning to Perth in November 1879, he had set the stage for a hero's homecoming. From the far northern port of Darwin he telegraphed ahead, describing 'twenty million acres of well-watered country' which, he said, was equal to the best grazing land in Australia. To some there was an ominous and hollow familiarity about Forrest's report. Had not Grey, Panter, Gregory and others said the same things about their northern explorations? Memories of the failed pastoral ventures – Camden Harbour, Denison Plains and Roebuck Bay – haunted the minds of the more conservative.

This time it would be different. The new lands boasted abundant water and captured the imagination of Western Australian colonists. At last, someone had returned home with news of the much-promised northern El Dorado that would propel the struggling colony into economic prosperity. Grey and those who followed him in the Camden Harbour fiasco had gone to the wrong place. But now, Forrest had shown the way to the Fitzroy and Ord river valleys, which held the key to future northern prosperity. This would be the economic heart of the Kimberley.

Like a conquering military leader returning from distant battle, Forrest arrived in Perth to scenes of public acclamation. Most of Perth's six thousand residents lined the streets to bask and share in his glory as a horse-drawn open carriage circled the town. Later in the day, at a civic reception in his honour, Forrest was praised by the Governor, with other public officials and prominent colonists, to an audience that overflowed the Town Hall.

Twice before, Alexander Forrest had been on long exploration journeys under the command of his elder brother John, who had enjoyed previous public accolades. John advanced rapidly in the government service and in 1879 held the position of Acting Commissioner for Crown Lands. Now Alexander held centre stage, and with his brother looking on, boasted to the Town Hall crowd: 'I hope and trust that before many years are over, the country we have discovered will be the home of a large population, as I feel certain that it is some of the finest country in Australia.' Injecting an element of patriotism, Forrest claimed, 'This magnificent country for pasture is certainly a great acquisition to this colony and colonists only have themselves to blame if they allow outsiders to come and monopolise it.'[5]

Yet personal greed appeared to outweigh any loyalty Forrest had for Western Australia. Anticipating the public response to his report, he soon resigned as contract surveyor to the Lands Department and established himself as an entrepreneurial land agent, canvassing throughout Australia for prospective Kimberley investors. Publicity surrounding his expedition triggered an unprecedented land boom dubbed 'Kimberley fever' by the press.

The new lands could not be taken up until early 1881, when the Government gazetted the much-awaited Kimberley Land Regulations. A so-called 'stocking clause', designed to deter land speculators, was inserted. The clause, requiring would-be squatters to stock a minimum of two cattle or twenty sheep per thousand acres, deterred many Western Australian settlers from taking up leases in the new district because they didn't have the finances to meet the lease conditions. It did not deter the land speculators from eastern Australia and Britain who could afford the risk. Of 448 initial requests for Kimberley land, the Lands Department leased eight million acres to fifty-five successful applicants. By the end of 1882, more than forty-four-million acres had been granted to seventy-seven people. Yet one third of the total area leased went to only five people. The vast majority of the Kimberley soon fell into the hands of Sydney and Melbourne-based speculators. For many investors the Kimberley was a gamble; most had no intention of stocking their runs but planned to sell out to make handsome profits at a later date.

Prominent Western Australian colonists protested loudly that eastern Australian speculative greed made Kimberley leases unaffordable. The Kimberley was promised to Western Australians but the only beneficiaries were eastern capitalists, they said. Yet Frederick Napier Broome had no reservations about the speculative activity when he began his tenure as governor in early 1883. The more speculation the better, he thought. In a despatch to new Secretary of State Lord Derby, Broome described the Kimberley as a 'gold mine'. Indeed it was! For the first time in its history, the Western Australian Colony in 1883 recorded a surplus of revenue made possible through renting unstocked Kimberley leases.

As the deadline to stock the leases approached, colonists with a commitment to live or employ station managers in the region emerged. Various consortiums and family interests sent survey parties to the Kimberley in 1881 and 1882, foreshadowing the two types of pastoral industry that would occupy the region. The eastern Kimberley mountainous terrain and fertile river valleys were ideally suited to open cattle grazing. Pastoralists from Queensland and New South Wales, the most prominent of whom was the Durack family, overlanded their stock and established their cattle runs.

On the west side, pastoralists, predominantly from southern Western Australia, moved in with their flocks of sheep. Wool-growing suited this flat red-earth pindan country with its richly grassed pastures along the Fitzroy and Lennard Rivers. Both rivers flowed from Milawundi (King Leopold Range), a formidable line of mountains dividing the Kimberley conveniently into east and west.

The first Kimberley settlers ignored moral questions about usurping Aboriginal people from their land. Like soldiers embarking to fight 'a just war', they acted with the full blessing of their society. In nineteenth century Western Australia, the northern squatters were revered as pioneering crusaders, extending civilised order to the wilderness.

The Fitzroy River Valley, with its grassy plains, was the magnet that drew the sheep squatters. These were hardened young Western Australian-born men from the south-west of the colony, whose fathers and uncles had violently crushed Nyoongar communities and established sheep farms on their lands. The young men were employed by two consortiums, the Kimberley Pastoral Company and the Murray River Squatting Company, whose principal financial backer was prominent member of the Western Australian parliament, WE Marmion. They found themselves living in the midst of much larger Aboriginal populations than their fathers had experienced, and were determined to subdue them with terror. At the same time they were fearful that the Nyikina people who surrounded them were about to launch a full-scale attack on their two stations, Mt Anderson and Lower Liveringa.

In November 1882, Mt Anderson Station manager Anthony Cornish was speared to death by an old Nyikina man. Court testimony later revealed that Cornish had had a sexual relationship with the old man's wife. Yet personal provocation counted for nothing as the settlers demanded retribution. Cornish's good friend and manager of neighbouring Liveringa Station, J McLarty, wrote that the killing 'will have a bad effect on the settlement of this district as the blacks will think that a white man is easily overcome'.[6]

A police party quickly despatched from Roebourne hunted down the hapless old man. His fate had been determined even before he arrived in Perth to undergo the ritual of public trial. His young wife Naura was also shipped down as a Crown witness, to give the verdict credence. Through an interpreter she described her established sexual liaison with Cornish, prompting a vigorous cross-examination by the prosecution. She was pressured to agree that the killing had nothing to do with an aggrieved husband's honour, but was motivated by a treacherous will to steal sheep. Her husband was found guilty and, just days later, in view of an assembly of distressed, sick Aboriginal prisoners at Rottnest Island, the old man was hanged.

The old man's trial and execution were a triumphant display by government of 'British' justice being imposed on the Kimberley frontier. Designed more for the colonists than for Aborigines, the spectacle emphasised the righteousness of applying the principles of law and order to Aboriginal people who opposed pastoral occupancy. Cornish's death hastened the government's decision to appoint Robert Fairbairn as Kimberley Government Resident. Derby had already been named as the district's port and administrative centre and Fairbairn's immediate task was to choose a location for the township. Commanding a small police contingent, he had other roles: as Judge, Customs Officer and Registrar of Economic Statistics. On the Kimberley frontier, Fairbairn, who only a few years earlier had been an obscure public servant in Perth, now claimed greater powers than any other regional official in the colony.

Any romantic illusions Fairbairn may have had about performing like a governor in a new colony soon disappeared. Timber brought from Perth to build his residence was washed overboard and strewn for miles on the mosquito-infested mudflats that surrounded the site he had chosen for Derby. For months he lived in a makeshift tent, suffering from the searing heat and monsoonal rains while he awaited additional building supplies from Perth. Weak with fever and despairing, Fairbairn pleaded to be sent home. To back up his request he argued that a Kimberley Magistrate was not required in a district containing only six sheep stations, supporting fifty-two settlers and twenty-eight thousand sheep.

Broome was determined that this Kimberley settlement would not fail and angrily rejected Fairbairn's plea. Dismissing negative assessments of the Kimberley's sluggish growth, the Governor ordered Fairbairn to remain until his two-year term expired. With enthusiasm Broome wrote to Lord Derby, the new British Secretary of State for the Colonies, pointing out that although 'settlement has not yet begun', large numbers of stock were being marshalled to the Kimberley by way of overland drives from Queensland.[7]

While the Duracks and others were preparing to stock their East Kimberley leases with cattle, the large influx of permanent settlers so eagerly foreshadowed by Broome did not eventuate. Most of the settler activity centred on the sheep lands of the West Kimberley. By 1884, the lower Fitzroy country was occupied by Liveringa, Mt Anderson and Yeeda sheep stations, while other squatters established runs hastily on available land along the Lennard River, directly east of Derby.

The Government practically ignored pastoral occupation of the east Kimberley. Cattle-grazing was alien to Western Australians. Besides, it was felt that if there were money to be made from beef it would flow to the east, and not benefit the Western Australian colony. Only when gold was discovered in late 1885 did the government show interest in the east, quickly gazetting the towns of Wyndham and Halls Creek. It was in the wool-growing settlers of the west Kimberley that the Western Australian Government and its leading colonists put their faith.

The most colourful of these early settlers was William Lukin who, in early 1883, transported four thousand sheep to the Kimberley.

A tall man in his early thirties, Lukin possessed a raw enthusiasm unmatched by any other contemporary Kimberley settler. His capacity for hard work was legendary and, despite the harsh northern climate, he demanded similar efforts from his workers, black or white. He even sacked his own nephew, Henry Bostock, for returning late from Derby with station supplies.

A member of an established land-owning Western Australian family, William Lukin became embittered when his elder brother Lionel inherited the family property, Deepdale, near Toodyay in the Avon Valley. After establishing a small farm near Beverley with his younger brother George, William soon became bored. Excited by Alexander Forrest's Kimberley expedition, Lukin saw the chance to realise his dream to become a great landholder and breed race horses like a British aristocrat.

Lukin installed himself as landlord over a million acres of fertile Lennard River valley land. What he lacked in capital he made up in unbounded energy and managed to inspire JH Monger, the patriarch of another Avon Valley family, to back him financially. Naming his sheep-run Lennard River Station, Lukin became the envy of other Kimberley triers who saw his lease as a prize selection. The rich red pindan earth was well grassed and had ample water supplied by the Lennard River and numerous creeks and springs flowing from the nearby Balili. So fertile was the land that Lukin doubled his sheep numbers by natural increase within two years.

Lukin built his homestead above what he thought was the high-water flood mark of the Lennard River, ten miles from the Balili range. He saw this limestone wall of rock as a great asset for the water it provided and as a natural fence for his sheep. It was a near-impenetrable barrier, which stopped his sheep straying east into the rocky and hilly wilderness country stretching to Milawundi. Coloured gun-barrel grey, this extraordinary geological formation was once an ancient coral reef. Its sheer cliffs, rising at times to several hundred feet, contrasted powerfully with the flat red clay grasslands that stretched westward to the skyline. The range was less than half a mile wide over most of its length, but it presented a formidable ridge, snaking its way over several hundred miles of West Kimberley terrain.

Another early Kimberley pastoralist was Isadore Emanuel. He was to prove that one needed more than blind determination and the possession of fertile river valley pastures to succeed as a Kimberley grazier. Emanuel boasted a rare combination of skills: shrewd economic management and the ability to forge powerful economic and political alliances. The eldest son of a wealthy Jewish family from Goulburn, New South Wales, he was made responsible for trans- porting sheep to the family's West Kimberley holdings in 1884. First he attempted an overland drive to the Kimberley from the eastern seaboard, a distance without precedent in Australian wool-grazing history. This courageous endeavour ended in costly failure when drought halted the stock drive at the Durack family's cattle station at Coopers Creek in Queensland.

Despite the overland debacle, a determined Emanuel continued his efforts to get sheep to the Kimberley. Returning to Sydney he persuaded a number of the so-called Kimberley-map graziers to underwrite half the financial risk of shipping sheep around the treach- erous northern Australian coast to King Sound. He then purchased twelve thousand high-quality sheep from the wealthy New South Wales Riverina district and, during 1884 and 1885, transported them to the West Kimberley in four shipments.

There Emanuel began carving out a pastoral empire backed up by complex deals with Sydney-based financiers. The family first established a run on the Lennard River adjoining Meda Station, a site chosen because of its proximity to the sheep-landing area at Point Torment, north of Derby. Yet the area offered little room for expansion and in 1886 the property was surrendered when Emanuel transferred his rapidly growing flock to his Fitzroy holding, naming it Upper Liveringa.

This was to be the first acquisition in an expanding empire that would give him eventual control over much of the remaining Bandaral ngarri land. Next, Noonkanbah Station was added to Emanuel's growing landholdings. In the early 1890s, Emanuel centred his pastoral empire at Mt Campbell, where he built a homestead a few miles south of the junction of Bandaral ngarri and Mayalnga. Mt Campbell Station was a huge tract of land that later incorporated three separate pastoral leases; Go Go, Christmas Creek and Cherrabun.

The only other early settler to match Emanuel's economic expertise and financial backing was William Forrester, whose assault on the West Kimberley was meticulously planned. After conducting a thorough survey of the region in 1882, Forrester hurried to Perth to lodge his land selections with the Lands Department. He telegraphed his partner, James Munro, a wealthy Victorian investor and rising politician, with the news of his chosen land on the Upper Lennard River, describing it as the 'best he had seen in the Kimberley'.[8] With absolute confidence in Forrester's judgment, Munro established a public company, named it the King Sound Pastoral Company, and invited investors to inject capital into the venture. Interestingly, many of the shareholders had invested in the Camden Harbour fiasco almost twenty years before. However, this new corporate exercise in northern colonisation was totally different. The shareholders might not ever see their Kimberley holding but they provided capital so that the station could maximise wool production under Forrester's skilful management.

Munro was the largest shareholder in the company. Scottish by birth, he had become wealthy through a string of investments, including a controlling interest in the prestigious Melbourne Woollen Mills Company. Throughout the 1880s, he speculated wildly on the booming Melbourne real estate market until it collapsed in the early 1890s, sending his business and political career into oblivion. His pastoral interests extended to several Queensland cattle properties and, by the late 1880s, Munro was the wealthiest landowner in Australia. To fund his extravagant investments, Munro borrowed from the financial institutions he and other members of his family controlled.

Forrester, a scientific manager who experimented lavishly on expensive breeding programs designed to produce high-quality wool, could not have found a better financier. In late 1884, Forrester occupied his prized pastoral selection on land destined to become a focal point of violent conflict with the Bunuba owners.

The one million acre property, just like Lukin's Lennard River Station, which it bordered at its northern boundary, was divided by the Balili wall. The settlers saw the eastern side as a rocky, infertile wilderness, impossible for managing sheep, but they viewed the flat lands to the west as magnificent pasture. In the first half-yearly meeting held in Collins Street, Melbourne, the King Sound Pastoral Company directors congratulated themselves on having established the best sheep run in the Kimberley.

The directors' confidence in the economic future of the property was supported by the evidence. Like Lukin's adjoining station, the land contained a plentiful supply of year-round water and was heavily grassed. The many boab trees, referred to uncharitably by Forrester as the 'box tree', graced the surrounding landscape and provided sheep with much needed shade. The property's fertility far exceeded that of Lukin's because it contained the valued Galanganyja plains, on which grew the most luxuriant grasses. Forrester, who had had previous pastoral experience in the wealthy grazing district of western Victoria, assessed his station's carrying capacity at sixty thousand sheep and claimed to be managing the 'best pastoral land in Australia'.[9]

Forrester chose for his homestead a site of serenity and beauty. It lay in the shadows of the Balili, where a gently meandering stream flowed from a spring within a cave at the foot of the cliff-face. At the entrance to the cave stood a tall tree with leafy, out-reaching branches adorned by yellow fig-like fruit. The Bunuba people, who belonged to the country Forrester now claimed, called the tree Limalurru. Forrester mispronounced it 'Lillimooloora', a name which he adopted officially for the whole of his pastoral property.

Lillimooloora and Lennard River stations enjoyed a short-lived status as the Kimberley's showpiece squatting runs. In their supreme arrogance, Lukin and Forrester had not seriously considered that the Bunuba people might resist their presence. The new landholders had selected their pastoral runs largely because of the economic advantages afforded to them by the limestone escarpment. Never did they anticipate that the Bunuba would maintain the basis of an independent society and resist the settlers through a strategic advantage offered by that same limestone range. A wall of rock defined the boundary of pastoral-held land and Aboriginal-held land.

This lasted until the late 1890s. The Aboriginal people of the West Kimberley flat-lands were overrun. Without a mountainous retreat they were hunted down by pastoralists and police. Within a few years, most Aboriginal people inhabiting the coastal and lower Lennard and Bandaral ngarri river areas had surrendered their independence, eventually to become servants of the pastoralists. However, the Balili range allowed the Bunuba to come and go from Limalurru and Lennard River stations as they wished.

By 1885, Lukin was expressing doubts about the strategic location of his station. The independent Aboriginal people who made inquisitive and fleeting visits to his homestead infuriated him. He had enough trouble maintaining the loyalty of a small assembly of white workers and found it almost impossible to recruit a servile

Aboriginal workforce. At the inaugural meeting of the Kimberley Pastoral Association, which elected Forrester chairman and Emanuel secretary, Lukin expressed bitterness about his labour difficulties. He put a motion, seconded by Emanuel, that 'the laws for the punishment of aborigines should be altered so that flogging might be resorted to as the penalty for absconding aboriginal assigned servants'.[10]

At the same meeting Emanuel called for the appointment of six West Kimberley settlers as justices of the peace. The motion was unanimously adopted and he followed it with a strongly worded letter to Governor Broome. Fairbairn intervened and advised Broome that the West Kimberley settlers could not be trusted with judicial powers. 'Far from receiving assistance from the settlers who seem anxious to be placed on the Commission of the Peace,' Fairbairn argued, 'I feel that the Government Resident would be seriously impaired in the discharge of magisterial duties.'[11] Fairbairn's advice was accepted. The Broome administration believed the best way to maintain peace in the Kimberley was to concentrate judicial might in the hands of one trusted government resident.

With disdain the settlers claimed Fairbairn was more interested in protecting the Aboriginal people than in supporting them. Fairbairn had drawn such condemnation because of his strict adherence to the government's policy of not issuing warrants for the capture of Aboriginal people on the fringes of pastoral settlement. Without warrants there was little police activity on outlying stations.

In the late 1880s, no other government resident in Western Australia held such powerful dominance over the district of his jurisdiction. The appointment of strategically placed justices of the peace in the Gascoyne, Murchison, Ashburton and North West districts had distributed judicial powers to the settlers. With the backing of the 1883 Aboriginal Offenders Act these newly titled squatters held sweeping powers over Aboriginal people. Not only could they issue warrants to the police but they were empowered also to convict and sentence Aborigines to prison terms of up to six months and order whippings of fifty lashes.

Governor Broome decided that the sheep graziers in the Kimberley could not be trusted with these powers. His prime responsibility as governor was to steer Western Australia to political independence from Britain. Successful colonisation of the Kimberley was a key factor in the move toward Western Australian self-government. The British Government was already deeply concerned about reports of northern settler violence against Aboriginal people and the wide-spread allegations of slavery in the pearling and pastoral industries. Broome was convinced that Kimberley pastoralists would use judi-cial powers if they were granted them to engage in massive violence against Aboriginal people and thus jeopardise the opportunity for the British Government to grant political independence to Western Australian colonists.

Delighted to be rid of Fairbairn at the expiry of his term in late 1885, the ragged band of West Kimberley settlers looked forward to greater support from his replacement, Dr Thomas Lovegrove. Combining the functions of government resident and district medical officer, Lovegrove was particularly welcome because of the debilitating prevalence of tropical fever in the district. Yet over time, Lovegrove's relationship with settlers and police soured considerably. The issue again was the treatment of Aboriginal people, and more specifically, the question of how the authorities should deal with the Bunuba people who had shown an obvious determination to defend their homelands.

CONFLICT

IN MID-1885 AN ANGRY BUNUBA group confronted two prospective pastoralists, Baird and Morrison, near Gunbi, a little to the east of the Balili range. Waving spears, the Bunuba demanded that the settlers leave their country. With guns firing, the frightened would-be pastoralists retreated, never to return to the lease they had won by ballot a few years earlier. The incident highlighted the souring relations between the Bunuba and settlers.

Lukin and Forrester had met no such challenge when they first arrived with their sheep. In fact they received initial hospitality and assistance from the Bunuba and neighbouring Unggumi people. Both sides wanted peace, although the early contact was guarded and tentative. Lukin and Forrester could not afford conflict with the actual owners of the lands they now saw as theirs. They and their small group of workers were heavily outnumbered by the Bunuba. For Lukin especially, amicable relations offered an opportunity to recruit desperately needed black workers.

Forrester attempted to develop a friendship with the Bunuba who, he believed, would show him the country and waterholes for his sheep, which were being shipped in ever growing numbers. He was guided to important places such as Bandilngan, Barralama and Marawan. Forrester accorded them their Aboriginal names, which was rare recognition on the Kimberley frontier. Some he got hopelessly wrong.

Bandilngan, a short walk from Forrester's Lillimooloora homestead, was a place of supreme importance to the Bunuba. Here the Lennard River had cut a spectacular passage through the Balili range. For thousands of years the Bunuba and their Unggumi neighbours had used the gorge for ceremonies; they also fished and swam in the permanent pools of water. Creation heroes were painted on the limestone walls and the small caves high up on the gorge walls were the memorials for thousands of Bunuba dead whose skeletons were wrapped carefully in paperbark. The Bunuba told Forrester of the importance of the gorge and described it as Wandjina, the name for sacred places in this area. Forrester's misnaming of the gorge was an insult to its spiritual power and misleading to the white people, who would much later come in their tens of thousands to bask in the wonder of the place.

The Bunuba sought goodwill for obvious reasons. They were also interested in the settlers' material goods and food. However, they soon saw these strange people with their sunburnt red faces as ignorant and arrogant, disrespectful of the law of the land. They had to be taught that serious injury or possible death would follow should sacred sites be desecrated. Women, old men and children were at first shielded while two mature and confident men were chosen to act as intermediaries with the strangers from Lillimooloora homestead. Two of these men, Ellemarra and Packer, were seen as leaders.

Exuding a welcoming spirit, they were embraced by the settlers. Tall men, with a gregariousness that softened the image created by their muscular, ceremonially-scarred bodies, they quickly won the trust of the isolated newcomers. Forrester and his workers soon felt relaxed and secure among these physically powerful but disarming men. However, the settlers misread their situation completely. A year later Bunuba people, led by Packer and Ellemarra, would threaten the very existence of the Lillimooloora homestead.

When the settlers would not share their goods, the Bunuba simply took them. Lukin's and Forrester's homesteads and out-camps were constantly pillaged. Young Bunuba hunters prized glass, because the thick base of a bottle was flinted easily, then shaped into a potentially deadly spearhead. Soon this procedure superseded the tedious practice of manufacturing spearheads from quartz. The Bunuba ingeniously adapted other items, such as axes, billycans and bags of flour. On one occasion, Forrester encountered a hastily deserted Bunuba encampment and was amazed to find many of his own pieces of equipment scattered about.

The settlers saw the Bunuba use of their goods and chattels as theft and became increasingly embittered. When Bunuba raiders took a two-hundred-pound bag of flour from a station out-camp, a showdown loomed. The settlers decided that they had to teach the Bunuba a lesson. Soon afterwards, in June 1885, Cairns, one of Forrester's workers, shot and wounded Ellemarra as he walked casually from the Lillimooloora homestead with an assortment of station implements. It was a painful and bloody shotgun wound. Ellemarra would recover quickly from the wound, but relations between settlers and Bunuba would never recover.

By October 1885, goodwill had collapsed completely. The settlers reacted violently to the presence of Bunuba at their campsites, as on the occasion of the wounding of Ellemarra, but from the Bunuba perspective, it was the settlers' total disregard for special places that caused most alarm.

The settlers dismissed Bunuba warnings about the spiritual significance of certain places as primitive superstitions. If they had listened to the Bunuba and respected their cultural sites, many of the violent clashes could have been avoided. But cultural arrogance prevailed time and time again. Forrester ordered that sheep-yards be erected at the base of a looming pylon of rock, which had broken away from the cliff-face at the entrance of Bandilngan. The rock was the daunting figure of the creation hero, Jula. Building sheep-yards here was inappropriate and disrespectful.

Yet Forrester would commit a far more heinous crime at a place nearby, which exudes immense spiritual power and beauty. A remarkable geological formation, it breaks out of the limestone ranges to form a large, circular amphitheatre. Where the ring of rock meets the Balili range cliff-face, there lies a deep, clear pool fed by permanent spring water. To Forrester, the site was a superb natural enclosure for his sheep. To the Bunuba, it was sacred, a place where two dogs, creation heroes, after travelling over vast distances, ended their journey tragically. In a vain attempt to find water, the dogs dug deep into the ground, scattering large rocks around the hole. Their legacy is the clear bluewater rock pool and a powerful guide to moral behaviour. The Bunuba used the flat ground in front of the pool for important ceremonies. This was hallowed land. Its use for sheep-grazing could not be tolerated.

One day, having completed their sacrilegious work, the Lillimooloora stockmen were attacked by a Bunuba group led by Packer as they returned to the homestead. Under a shower of spears, the settlers fired shots as they fled the angry mob. They were followed by an axe-wielding Packer and his comrades, who gestured aggressively that the settlers should not return. At the time of this attack, smoke rose from the Balili plateau, signalling a simultaneous raid on Lillimooloora homestead, carried out by Ellemarra and three other Bunuba men. A spear took the station cook in the arm but he was able to fire his gun to fend off the attackers.

The next day, Forrester accompanied his stockmen to Bandilngan to search for the assailants. Halfway into the deep gorge, the settlers were startled to find their passage blocked by a large mob, armed with hardwood clubs and shovel-blade spears, defiantly holding their ground. Forrester, firing his revolver, hit a young man named Jilbara in the legs. Quickly, the band dispersed and, scaling both sides of the gorge walls, hurled rocks down on the settlers. One struck Forrester on the head. With blood streaming down his face, he ordered his men to retreat to the safety of the homestead.

Stunned by the unexpected aggression, Forrester assessed the situation as desperate and immediately sent word to Derby, requesting urgent police support. Within a week, police troopers McAltee and Ritchie, accompanied by two black troopers, arrived to survey the Bandilngan battle scene. They found the wounded Jilbara, but were satisfied with Forrester's explanation that he had been hit accidentally. Deciding not to concern themselves with the mass attack on Forrester's party, the police focused their attention on capturing Packer, Ellemarra and the others who had participated in the earlier clashes.

Two Bunuba guides led the police miles to the north. After days of searching, the troopers were convinced that they had been misled and returned to Lillimooloora. Through skilled deception like this, the Bunuba frustrated police and settlers on many occasions.

Undeterred, the stubborn police continued to scour the area around Bandilngan. A number of Bunuba watched the futile search from nooks and crevices in the limestone range, becoming increasingly impatient at the continued police presence. Then two more Bunuba men stepped forward and volunteered as guides, convincing the police that this time they would be led to the wanted men. The police posse was guided through thirty miles of spectacular but hazardous country. Sometimes they rode but mostly they walked over the red granite hills and through the beautiful Lennard and Richenda River valleys.

The journey took three days until finally, suffering exhaustion and blistered feet, they halted at the base of Gunbi. Rising sharply to almost four thousand feet, Gunbi is the highest mountain in sight and forms part of the great Kimberley divide – the Milawundi range. Here the police were told that the men were camped on the other side of the mountain.

Exasperated, the troopers conceded defeat and embarked wearily on the return journey to Derby. Near Lillimooloora, Ellemarra approached the police confidently, not knowing that they carried a warrant for his arrest on a charge of stealing flour. He was chained immediately and padlocked around the neck, becoming the first Bunuba to be arrested and transported by force from his country.

Shortly afterwards, Forrester was struck down by fever. In a delirious state he attempted desperately to seek medical help from Lovegrove in Derby but managed only to reach Lennard River Station where he died in Lukin's arms. To the settlers, Forrester's illness was the legacy of being drenched a week or so earlier when off-loading sheep at Pt Torment. But to the Bunuba, it was without doubt the work of their unpardoning laws.

Meanwhile, in Derby, Ellemarra was sentenced to six months' imprisonment. At the time, the tiny administrative town had no prison and short-term prisoners were secured in ad hoc fashion. Like other Aboriginal prisoners who were sentenced for six months or more, Ellemarra was transported by sea to Roebourne where up to sixty prisoners at a time were crowded into a stone prison. These prisoners laboured in chains, constructing roads and public buildings for long hours in the sun. By manual labour they built the twenty-mile-long causeway and tram-track linking Roebourne to its port at Cossack across the parched saltbush flats.

It was here on the causeway that Ellemarra, with only one month of his sentence remaining, made a daring escape by severing his chain with a prison-issue pickaxe. His dash for freedom was a cleverly planned manoeuvre. He knew that a former Lillimooloora stockman,

Robert Allen, was shortly leaving Roebourne to overland sheep to Oobagooma Station north of Derby. Ellemarra hid in the bush for some time, then with disarming charm approached Allen with an offer to help shepherd the flock. Allen, who knew Ellemarra, readily accepted. With astonishing ease Ellemarra had arranged an armed escort through foreign and dangerous country, and within weeks was enjoying the freedom of his homeland.

Ellemarra's escape was a critical political matter confronting Lovegrove when he assumed his Kimberley command in mid-1886. He feared the escape would erode Aboriginal people's deference to colonial rule. What Lovegrove and the settlers wanted was a cowering, subject people. Accordingly, a police patrol consisting of Constables Ritchie and Farrell and two black troopers was quickly despatched to recapture the escapee. They located him camped with a number of his countrymen near Lukin's homestead. The troopers charged on horseback, killing a young man and injuring others. The elusive Ellemarra escaped and when the police followed, he turned on them defiantly, hurling a spear which grazed Farrell's shoulder and knocked him from his horse.

Bruised and shaken, Farrell and the others returned to Derby empty-handed but with alarming information about the impact of Ellemarra's liberation. Ellemarra had apparently travelled widely among Aboriginal groups, boasting of his escape and engendering contempt for the settlers and police. Ritchie reported to his superiors, '. . . Ellemarra tells the blacks that the white man is no good and the blackfellow should not be afraid of them.'[1] A disturbed Lovegrove demanded that the Derby Police Chief dispatch his mounted troopers again to secure Ellemarra's arrest.

Official determination to recapture Ellemarra was used by the police as justification of their attempt to crush growing Bunuba dissidence through indiscriminate killing. Two patrols to the Balili range in quick succession shot a number of Bunuba people near Lillimooloora homestead. Ellemarra was not captured but the police created such intense hostility that relations were now irretrievably bad.

In October 1886, a third police patrol led by Ritchie was ordered to the Balili range. Near the Lennard River the men came upon a sizeable Bunuba encampment. Alerted to the imminent police attack, possibly by a black cockatoo, later referred to by Aborigines as the 'police bird', some thirty Bunuba dispersed, fleeing to the cover of the limestone ranges. In the confusion Ritchie became isolated in a rocky ravine and found himself confronted by an old man, Tarrodie, angrily brandishing a spear. Ritchie fired his rifle, wounding Tarrodie in the arm, but the determined old man continued to bear down on the terrified policeman. When Ritchie's rifle jammed he panicked, firing ineffectively from his revolver before police reinforcements arrived and shot the old man dead.

Tarrodie's horrified relatives saw the slaying from the safety of the Balili plateau. Soon, the bemused police watched several of the Bunuba running backward and forward, shaking their spears in powerless emotional gestures. They showered rocks down on the police, who countered with gunfire, hitting a young Bunuba lad named Lambardoo. The stunned Bunuba were silenced as the boy fell over two hundred feet to his death.

In an instant, the cliffs were bare and not a person was to be seen. It was as though the Bunuba had come to realise that confrontation with those who possessed the deadly firearm was suicidal. The police also departed, and Ritchie noted in his journal that the Bunuba could not be captured in the limestone range country. 'The only way to shift them is with a gun,' he said, 'and that would take many men.' He also reported that the whole of Lillimooloora Station was 'generally under siege'.[2]

Lovegrove was furious with the police performance in the outlying pastoral areas. He read Ritchie's journal with despair and immediately ordered police activity to halt in the Balili except in cases of emergency. In an acidic memorandum to Inspector Finnerty, recently appointed to head the police force in the Kimberley, Lovegrove claimed the police had caused many Aboriginal deaths but with 'little effect with regards their respect for the white man's authority or power'.[3] The order precipitated a constitutional crisis in Kimberley colonial authority.

As resident magistrate, Lovegrove considered himself the senior government officer. He reminded his subordinate of this by regular interference in police administration, often on the most petty matters. For weeks, the two were embroiled in acrimony until the point was reached when Lovegrove ordered Finnerty's arrest. The police officers remained loyal to their inspector. The settlers sided with the police and Lovegrove was isolated. At a public meeting in Derby they demanded the removal of Lovegrove, whom they claimed was 'unfit to carry out the duties of the Government Resident'.[4]

The conflict went far beyond a personal dispute. It centred on the vexed question of when and how to use armed force against Aboriginal people. Finnerty favoured the use of violence against those who defended their country against encroaching pastoral settlements. Lovegrove's approach was more in line with the law, which prohibited the indiscriminate slaughter of Aboriginal people. The Perth Government moved to resolve the Derby crisis by promoting Finnerty to the position of mining warden in Halls Creek.

Yet Finnerty's transfer solved nothing. The new Kimberley police chief, Sub-inspector Lodge, also supported the wholesale use of armed force against those who resisted. The chance to demonstrate military force was soon handed to Lodge when a settler named Piton was killed by an Aboriginal mob near the mouth of the Robinson River, north of Derby. Lodge led a large punitive expedition, which included settlers sworn in as special constables, to avenge Piton's death. He used this opportunity to make a wide sweep of the West Kimberley hill country and at the same time put down the Bunuba menace.

The police expedition was a total failure, particularly in Bunuba country. Lodge returned to Derby disappointed that he had not shot or captured any Aboriginal people. Not one Bunuba was seen by the police, despite the sighting of fresh footprints, hot campfire coals and hastily-discarded food. Their country, with its limestone ranges riddled with caves and chasms, swallowed up people as though they were ghosts. The Bunuba had obviously decided that contact with the police should be avoided.

Clearly, the Bunuba saw basic divisions in settler society. To them it was a weird world devoid of women and children. They called the settlers Malngarri, meaning red persons. The Bunuba distinguished police troopers from the other settlers and named them Darrali: literally, agitated king brown snake. In their physical world before white occupation, the angry king brown was the gravest threat to safety. So much for the Kimberley police as independent peacemakers protecting both settlers and Aborigines. The Bunuba quickly recognised the police, not the settlers, as their greatest threat.

Bunuba groups soon developed an intelligence system providing a measure of safety from attack. It largely centred on those old people and young women who, living around station homesteads, could relay messages to their relatives in the hills about settler and police movements. The so-called bush telegraph, often using hand and smoke signals, could transfer accurate information rapidly over vast distances.

Embarrassed by police failure in Bunuba country, Lodge blamed his black trackers, branding them incompetent cowards. The West Kimberley trackers, officially known as police native assistants, were recruited from Roebourne prison. It was normal practice to bring trackers from distant places. In this way police were generally assured of the trackers' loyalty and their readiness to confront foreign Aboriginal people as enemies.

The term 'tracker' is one of the great misnomers in Australian history. They were armed black troopers, who were vital to police search-and-destroy operations. Their multi-faceted role included locating food and water, gathering intelligence, either by stealth or torture, and guiding police troopers to Aboriginal encampments. Evidence of Aboriginal presence such as a footprint, a freshly broken tree branch or even a distant smell, unnoticeable to European senses, was detected by black troopers. Often, a single footprint revealed the critical information about sex, age and even the identity of people being pursued.

At the point of conflict, black tracker became black trooper. Frequently with guns blazing, they engaged zealously in the chase, capture and killing of hunted Aboriginal menfolk, usually as their police commanders supervised from a safe distance.

Conscripted Roebourne black troopers feared the Bunuba and avoided contact with them. As a result, police operations were ineffective. The police changed policy and for the first time used local Aborigines as black troopers. They were two young Bunuba prisoners, Lilamarra and Woorunmurra, called Jacky and Dicky by the police. They operated at first in Warrwa country, directly north of Derby, and were held in high regard by their police masters. But then Lodge tried to tighten the screws on the Bunuba and switched the troopers to fight against their own people. Now it was a different story. They led the police away from their families' encampments or gave black station workers information about police movements, which was transferred quickly to Bunuba people in the hills. Contrary to police expectations, Lilamarra's and Woorunmurra's police role expanded the established Bunuba intelligence system and enhanced their security.

It did not take long for the settlers to realise the police folly. In mid-1888, Isadore Emanuel, who had replaced Forrester as Chairman of the Kimberley Pastoral Association, argued that the police should revert to conscripting black troopers from distant places. It was common knowledge, he claimed, that Lilamarra and Woorunmurra would protect their relatives. The leader of the Kimberley pastoralists described the Bunuba as 'exercising a pernicious influence' upon the young black troopers. Emanuel wrote sternly to the colonial secretary that the only way to combat the Bunuba was to base police patrols permanently in areas of the disturbances. The Derby police were 'hopeless' against the Bunuba, he argued, because by the time patrols arrived at Lillimooloora and Lennard River stations, the stock killers had fled safely to the hills.[5]

Emanuel's comments reflected a growing frustration among West Kimberley pastoralists about sheep losses attributed to Aboriginal attacks. The Bunuba called sheep Gugunja, which evoked images of stupid woolly animals. Described in contemporary colonial language as 'native depredations', the killing of sheep was not indiscriminate plunder motivated simply by changes in dietary preference. For a community in flight, it was necessary to seize upon a readily available food supply. Critical factors determined that mutton was incorporated quickly into the Bunuba diet.

Bunuba society had been altered profoundly by European contact, which included pastoral activity, police patrols and gold fossicking. An important aspect of this traumatic period of first contact was the surrendering of camping and recreation sites because of their vulnerability to attack. To avoid the police and settlers, small Bunuba groups became highly mobile. Camping and eating places were often strategically located high on the Balili plateau, making it sometimes necessary to carry water. The Bunuba were forced to adapt and did so ingeniously. The easily procured sheep became a ready food source for a people on the run.

The settlers referred to Bunuba sheep killers as stock spearers, but sheep were also killed by other means. One captured Bunuba described in court the simple process of scampering down the limestone cliff-face and grabbing the stupid Gugunja with bare hands as they slept in the shade of the midday sun. Another prisoner told of constructing makeshift yards where many sheep were killed quickly.

The strategic lighting of fires, which destroyed fencing and stock, hit some of the stations hard. Aboriginal people were adept in the use of fire, which formed part of the tactical armoury of hunting and, more importantly, was a crucial method of environmental management. This was observed by Lukin in a rare acknowledgement by a settler of the worth of Aboriginal traditional practice. At a meeting of the Kimberley Pastoral Association in 1886, Lukin opposed a motion to outlaw Aboriginal people lighting fires on pastoral-held land. He claimed that the damage caused by fire was insignificant in comparison with the beneficial effects of pasture regeneration. Within two years, his opinion had altered after several hundred of his own sheep had perished in scrub fires. Then Lukin himself advocated the banning of fires deliberately lit by traditional owners.

Five years on, the Kimberley frontier had made Lukin an increasingly desperate man. His dream of achieving financial success and respectability had soured, largely because of the persistent and increasing Bunuba attacks on his station. In 1888, he agitated loudly for additional police support. In that year alone, Lukin claimed, he had lost two thousand sheep to Aboriginal attacks and he signalled his intention to abandon the country if the depredations continued. In a letter to a Perth paper, the *Western Mail*, he defended his position with a rhetorical question: 'Who is responsible for the dispossession of the natives? The government who receives the rent for the land, or the lessee who occupies the country with the full consent of the government?'[6]

Lukin's question was the familiar defence of the pastoralists turned into attack on the government. The pastoral lessees, Lukin and others argued, did not own the land but in a sense were the government's agents, utilising the land economically for the benefit of the wider community. They concluded that they were therefore entitled to receive adequate police support to subdue and dispossess the traditional owners of the land they fought to occupy.

In Perth, Governor Broome's administration continued to be influenced by Fairbairn's 1882 report which dismissed similar arguments by the pastoralists in the Gascoyne and Murchison districts. The relationship between sheep-graziers and Aboriginal people in these areas was similar to that in the Bunuba lands, except that desert, not a limestone escarpment, defined the boundary between Aboriginal-held and pastoral-occupied country. Gascoyne and Murchison pastoralists demanded that the government send police as troops to embark on a military campaign of mass slaughter against the Aborigines. The intention was to bring about the permanent subjugation of the traditional owners through terror and the creation of a servile labour force.

Instead, the colonial authorities sent up Fairbairn, then a trusted public servant in the Colonial Secretary's Office, to report on the situation. Fairbairn's report criticised the pastoralists for not employing white workers and relying on unpaid Aboriginal workers, who were needed in large numbers to manage sheep on expansive unfenced arid lands. Aboriginal shepherds came and went from the properties, often taking sheep back to their family camps or leaving them to die of thirst among the spinifex. These squatters could never afford to pay the wages needed to attract white shepherds to these hot lands and their economic survival depended totally on enslaving Aboriginal workers. Fairbairn also reported on the widespread sexual abuse of Aboriginal women by the squatters, which he said may have been one of the reasons Aboriginal workers so often returned to their independent homelands. Fairbairn's report was well crafted, by an ambitious civil servant who knew exactly what the government wanted to receive.

Race relations on the margins of colonial settlement highlighted the political balancing act that Perth colonial authority executed as Western Australia edged closer and closer to political independence. The colony had to meet two conditions to gain self-government. Firstly, it had to raise sufficient revenue from internal economic activity and not rely on funds from the imperial treasury in London. Secondly, it needed to demonstrate that the rule of law prevailed throughout the colony and that Aboriginal people, as British subjects, were not ill-treated. The police force was supposed to be an independent institution which protected both settlers and Aborigines. For the police to be used as a military force in an act of war against Aboriginal people on the pastoral frontier would surely have endangered any chance of liberating Western Australia from direct British rule.

So here was the dilemma. The only way that Perth colonial authorities could increase their own revenue was to lease out more and more pastoral land. Yet how were they to respond when the Aboriginal owners of the land resisted pastoral occupation and the servitude demanded by the settlers. In the eastern Gascoyne and Murchison they despatched a party of police, which travelled around the newly-established stations, capturing Aboriginal men en masse. The troopers were followed by a travelling magistrate named Voss who tried and sentenced all those captured to three years imprisonment. In 1883, several hundred Aboriginal men from the Gascoyne and Murchison districts were chained and herded like cattle to the coast and then transported to the cold and windswept Aboriginal prison of Rottnest Island, a few miles off the coast of Perth. There they died in large numbers and were buried in unmarked graves.

The dynamics on the frontier at the Lillimooloora homestead were different from those in the Gascoyne and Murchison, although the politics were the same. The King Sound Pastoral Company had invested heavily in fencing, thus reducing its dependence on labour. It also had the finances to employ the white workers needed, until such time as Aboriginal people could be induced to work in exchange for flour and tobacco. Yet in 1888, Lillimooloora Station reported that over four thousand sheep, nearly one third of its total flock, had been destroyed by the Bunuba. Gunn, who replaced Forrester as Munro's manager, returned to Melbourne late that year, a disillusioned and defeated man. His successor, Martin, presided over the economic ruin of a station at one time expected to be the best in Australia.

In late 1888, a public rally in Derby endorsed the demands of Lukin, Emanuel and others for police parties to be stationed permanently in outlying areas. The government, convinced that police troopers would be used as armed agents of the settlers, ordered Sergeant Sherry of Derby to provide an on-the-spot report. Sherry's role was similar to Fairbairn's six years earlier. His report, canvassed widely in the Perth press, concluded that only some stock losses were the responsibility of Aboriginal people. Dingoes and poisonous grass were other factors but, as Sherry remarked, it was customary among Kimberley sheep owners to blame all losses on Aborigines. Repeating Fairbairn's observations, he wrote that practically all stations were short-handed, highlighting lack of supervision as the major reason for stock losses. Singling out Lukin's property as the worst managed in the district, he claimed that the sheep on Lennard River Station were scattered over a wide area and appeared totally unshepherded.

Sherry conceded the impossibility of police confronting the Bunuba in the Balili range country. 'They will occasionally show themselves in the hills,' he wrote, 'but unless they are surprised in the open they cannot be taken.' Periodic police visits were futile as 'they retire to the security of the hills but return to their old haunts when the police have gone'.[7] He recommended that the only course possible was to station police troopers permanently in the contested areas. The government ignored this recommendation but used Sherry's findings to blame settlers for stock losses and delayed committing troops to the Kimberley frontier.

The West Kimberley settlers felt betrayed by their government's refusal to reinforce and decentralise the district's police. Branding Sherry's comments as libellous, the settlers launched a public attack on the police. In a letter to a Perth newspaper, a number of land-holders assailed the local troopers as incompetent. 'Nearly every prisoner has been either captured by the settlers or owes his capture to the settlers,' claimed the pastoralists with contempt.[8] Emanuel intensified the attack, publicly stating that the police were responsible for the lawlessness. He described them as 'an inefficient and incapable body of men . . . so much so that both settlers and blacks have thorough contempt for them'. Inspector Lodge emerged from the attack unscathed. Emanuel said it was not his fault that he had to administer an unworkable Aboriginal Law with men unfit to be police officers.[9]

The so-called Aboriginal Law was not a law as such but a British colonial legal principle, which held that Aboriginal people, as British subjects, should receive protection. Kimberley settlers believed that the application of this principle by magistrates and police was incon-sistent with their own commercial interests. The settlers demanded abolition of the system of issuing warrants because it gave the resident magistrate inordinate power over police operations. This was the government's intention, but Lukin argued that the system had become unworkable in the Lillimooloora area. Forrester's death and Gunn's departure had invalidated many warrants, thereby making it impossible legally to arrest several wanted Bunuba.

The settlers argued for the police to have broad 'discretionary powers', a term that became a popular political catchcry. It meant that police should be able to act without constraints from either the resident magistrate in Derby or police commissioner in Perth. Without apology the settlers saw the police as their servants, whose duty was to crush Aboriginal resistance without mercy. Settlers also sought the legal power to shoot certain Aboriginal people themselves. Lukin blamed the sheep-killing in the Balili range area on the elusive Ellemarra, whom he called the 'ringleader'. If the government allowed settlers the right to shoot the likes of Ellemarra, the trouble would soon be over, he contended.[10]

Governor Broome was not worried about sheep losses on the edge of settlement. During the debate about additional Kimberley police, he restated the dictum that stock-killing by Aborigines in isolated areas was not 'a serious crime'. He was more concerned about widespread conflict and wanton destruction of Aboriginal life and how that would be viewed in England.

Following revelations of settler and police atrocities in the East Kimberley and the widely held perception of the Kimberley as a lawless district, the government re-examined its position.

The Western Australian press entered the debate, demanding additional police. In a stinging editorial entitled 'Native Problems Exclusively Localised to the Kimberley', the *West Australian* argued that so-called 'Native Questions' —

> *must not be allowed to drift in the Kimberley till Western Australia's records become as stained as her eastern neighbours . . . It is for the Government to see that they do not . . . [the Government] cannot allow our colonists to be massacrers but on the other hand cannot allow insecurity to chase investors away.*[11]

It is debatable whether the argument was to protect the settlers against Aborigines or protect the Aborigines against the settlers. Either way, the pressure on the government to increase the Kimberley Police Force was overwhelming. In one of the last major political decisions ever made by a British Governor of Western Australia, Broome endorsed a Legislative Council motion to reinforce and decentralise the Kimberley Police Force. The motion, moved by James Lee Steere, read in part:

> *[it] is urgently desirable that strong and prompt measures should be taken for the protection of lives and property of the settlers in the Kimberley against the depredations of the natives now becoming alarmingly frequent and that as much of the whites as of the blacks a state of things should be prevented which if unchecked must eventually lead to guerilla warfare and regrettable reprisals.*[12]

The Kimberley police garrison, including black troopers, was increased to almost fifty. Inspector Lodge now commanded the most powerful police regiment in the colony. Reporting to the British Government, Broome claimed the force was strong enough to protect settlers and Aborigines and emphasised that settlers would not be signed on as special constables. Yet Police Commissioner Phillips showed signs of concern and implored Lodge to 'guard against excessive zeal or anything that looks like a campaign against the hill tribes.'[13]

In the West Kimberley, police were positioned at outposts on the Robinson River near Oobagooma Station and the Bandaral ngarri at Noonkanbah Station. The most sensitive outpost was at Lennard River near Bandilngan. Lodge considered it the most important in his district and appointed two hardened bushmen, William Armitage and Phillip Watts, to man it. They were assigned two black troopers, both recruited from the Pilbara district. For Lukin and Lillimooloora's manager Martin, the police presence was a godsend. They patrolled the area constantly, becoming familiar with Bunuba movements and encampments. With this knowledge the Lennard River police were able to surprise Bunuba encampments and, for the first time, Bunuba prisoners in large numbers were transported to the Derby prison.

In August 1889, the Lennard River troopers raided a Bunuba camp in the early hours of dawn in a vain attempt to capture Ellemarra. Amidst the chaos of fleeing people in the dim light, Armitage fired his gun indiscriminately, killing a boy named Jenulla. Armitage noted the event in his diary and mentioned it to Lodge who dismissed it as unimportant. Lovegrove, however, viewed the killing as illegal because there was no warrant for Jenulla's arrest. Preliminary evidence exonerated Watts but Lovegrove charged Armitage with murder and sent him to Perth to stand trial.

The West Kimberley settlers reacted in uproar. A strongly worded petition, undoubtedly penned by Lukin, and signed by forty-two settlers, demanded Armitage's release and a fundamental change to government policy in dealing with Aboriginal people on the Kimberley frontier. The petition called for 'the whole tribe of natives inhabiting Napier Range to be outlawed'.[14] The intention was to put the Bunuba people beyond the protection of the law. It would mean Aborigines in that area could be shot with impunity.

Only weeks from retirement, Broome predictably announced that no proceedings would be taken against Armitage. The young boy's death was regretted he said but the 'police were not to blame'. Predictably the settlers received no joy on the other point of the petition, which called for the outlawing of the Bunuba. 'Nothing like indiscriminate slaughter, as some settlers propose, can be permitted,' proclaimed the outgoing governor.[15]

The Perth press opposed outlawing the Bunuba people, whom they referred to as 'the hills tribe'. 'Nothing but the most intolerable conditions of danger could justify what would mean a war of extermination,' proclaimed the *Western Mail* in December 1889.[16] The paper expressed its support for the West Kimberley settlers, whom it described as 'brave and resolute men . . . laying the foundations of settlement in the most distant parts of the colony'. The paper urged the government to apply more vigorous police attention to quell Bunuba attacks on Lennard River and Lillimooloora stations. 'If the sword is to be unsheathed against the Aborigines it must be done by the properly constituted authorities,' the *Western Mail* proclaimed, with mediaeval righteousness.[17]

Armitage returned to his position at the Lennard River police camp and Lovegrove was transferred from Derby. Lovegrove, in constant conflict with the police since arriving in Derby in 1886, was too humanitarian for the emerging political order in Western Australia. On the eve of Western Australia's ascension to political independence, the government abandoned the practice of using the resident magistrate as a watchdog, to guard against settler and police aggression toward Aboriginal people in the West Kimberley. Lodge was chosen to replace Lovegrove and so combine the functions of police and judiciary. The Bunuba were now at the mercy of the police and settlers, who wanted all Aboriginal people ruthlessly shackled inside the fences of pastoral settlements.

THE LAND BETWEEN

THE BORDER SEPARATING BUNUBA-HELD LAND from those areas already colonised on behalf of the British Crown was not altered by the permanent stationing of police troopers at Lennard River. The Bunuba knew the country too well and held their ground against the small police presence. The police strategy was to constantly patrol on horseback and attack Bunuba encampments whenever they could. The invaders were confident that over time the Bunuba defences would crumble as young men were selectively wrenched from their homelands and put in chains.

Armitage, buoyed by having been granted immunity after killing Jenulla, was more determined than ever to engage the Bunuba. He and Watts, accompanied often by stockmen from the surrounding stations, made numerous raids into the Balili and Ganimbiri ranges and beyond. Becoming more familiar with Bunuba movements and encampment positions, the police knew when and where to attack. Earlier police patrols had frequently been comic failures but now Armitage and Watts employed clever tactics. Many a time, they worked under the cover of darkness, closing in on Bunuba campsites in readiness to attack at dawn. The Bunuba early warning system, once almost foolproof, began to crumble.

Mobility became critical to Bunuba survival. Often only the economically productive men could continue to live permanently in areas patrolled heavily by the police. Many of the women, children and old men were forced to live in feudal safety in the black camps near Lennard River and Lillimooloora station homesteads. They were in many instances accompanied by younger men who worked and resided temporarily on the stations.

By 1890, sizeable Aboriginal groups were attached to those homesteads. Aboriginal community was on the verge of social and economic collapse. In Western Australia's pastoral north, 'coming in', as it was known, occurred against a backdrop of violence. Nomadic parties learned that to stay in the bush was potentially suicidal, as marauding police and settlers hunted down Aboriginal people who refused to surrender their independence. The condition of surrender was that Aborigines received protection in exchange for servitude on pastoral holdings.

The Bunuba were not ready to surrender. Reunions for hunting, religious ceremonies and recreation occurred regularly, despite the social wounds that flowed from the break-up of family groups. The limestone bastion was the bulwark of Bunuba independence. Nowhere was a frontier between two opposing people more graphically demarcated. The journey from subservient station labour to Bunuba freedom could often be achieved in hours, or even minutes.

Lukin continued to complain vehemently about his 'floating' black workers. As long as the Bunuba retained an independent land base, the creation of a servile labour force was impossible. Like most other Kimberley settlers, Lukin did not bother indenturing black workers under the 1886 Aboriginal Protection Act. Instead, he laid criminal charges, mostly for sheep-killing, against Aboriginal men drifting from his station to the liberty of the ranges. Armed with a pile of warrants, police were legally entitled to act against a growing number of Bunuba men, often returning absconders to the station in chains. Many others made the chain-gang march to Derby prison.

The settlers possessed a siege mentality, an abiding fear that out beyond the limestone barrier were overwhelming numbers of Aboriginal people. The fear was reinforced by stock killings, bush-fires and the Balili barrier, which, like a magnet, drew the station blacks back to their homelands. The police and settlers had signalled they would not feel safe until this country had been surrendered. Yet conflict continued unresolved for many years because the battle-lines were blurred. The elusive Bunuba did not gather as one to face the invasion.

Individuals within that society responded in various ways to European occupation. While many refused to surrender their inde-pendence, others chose to cooperate. An increasing number drifted between the two societies. A few embraced the new colonial order. One extraordinary man, Jandamarra, ran the full gamut of Bunuba responses.

Jandamarra was only about six years old when Alexander Forrest and his party passed through Bunuba country in their failed attempt to link up with lands Grey had once explored. He would not have seen Forrest and his men in that August of 1879 because his family's country lay some miles westward of the explorer's path. His spirit-country on his father's side was the Bunuba homeland named Jumburr. Jumburr took in the section of the Balili plateau where most of the early conflict occurred between the Bunuba and settlers.

Rich in mythology and lore, it stretches southward from Bandilngan some twenty miles to where a waterway has carved a yawning cavity through the base of the Balili. The settlers named this awesome work of nature Tunnel Creek; the Bunuba referred to it as Baraa. Jandamarra would not learn the secret stories that told of the creation of his country and the law that flowed from it until he had reached puberty, the stage to commence formal education. Until then, he stayed with his mother, a powerful and independent woman who belonged to the northern Bunuba country of the Lennard River flat lands.

At about the age of eleven, Jandamarra came with his mother to live on Lennard River Station. No doubt Lukin welcomed the boy, who could be moulded into a productive pastoral worker far more readily than a man who by force of time was rooted deeply in his Aboriginal heritage. Superbly athletic, Jandamarra stood much shorter than his compatriots. Fully grown he was only five feet nine inches tall, well below the average Bunuba male height of over six feet. But what he lacked in height he made up for in running speed and agility. From these accomplishments Lukin dubbed him Pigeon, a name that, a few years later, would be emblazoned on the pages of every newspaper in the colony.

Before too long, Jandamarra drew praise as a pastoral worker. It took several years to mould the first generation of colonised Aboriginal labour before pastoralists came to rely on teams of black shearers. But very quickly Jandamarra became dexterous with the shearing blades, and his horsemanship was the envy of many. It was common for northern pastoralists to boast of their black stockmen's abilities, not so much for the qualities of the workers but in self-praise of their tutoring and management. In Jandamarra, Lukin believed he possessed the best black stockboy in the district.

But Jandamarra's real mentor was the unfortunately named Jim Crowe, another of Lukin's Aboriginal workers. Arriving in the Kimberley in 1883 as Lukin's servant, Crowe became the leading hand and at times the de facto manager of Lennard River Station. He had been arrested ten years earlier at Toodyay after killing another Aboriginal man in a drunken brawl. He was convicted of murder and sentenced to imprisonment on Rottnest Island, from where he was conscripted to Roebourne as a police assistant. Crowe became renowned as a trooper and was credited with the capture of many Aboriginal stock killers and escapees from pearling and pastoral masters.

John and Alexander Forrest seconded Jim Crowe as a guide on their 1878 north-west survey. Alexander Forrest was so impressed with Crowe's service that he requested the colonial secretary to remit his sentence. This angered the Roebourne police, who sought to retain the service of their best black trooper. Jim Crowe was released eventually and found his way back to his former life as servant on the Avon Valley property of the Lukin family.

At Lennard River Station Crowe's most important responsibility was to recruit Aboriginal workers, train them and supervise their labour. He became friends with Jandamarra, teaching him how to handle a horse and probably telling him about a life outside the Bunuba world. The most important skill Crowe taught him was how to use a gun. With revolver or rifle, Jandamarra soon became an uncanny marksman.

The gun, the embodiment of settler power over Aboriginal people, was, as Jandamarra came to understand it, simply a weapon to be used by anybody who possessed it. It may have been through his mastery of the firearm that Jandamarra came to look at the settlers' might as illusory and saw little reason to fear it. The settlers found him confident and exuberant, with a subtle charm, an endearing lad with unusual abilities, a recruit won over from the darkness of the wilderness.

Yet Jandamarra's loyalty to Lukin and Jim Crowe and his allegiance to Lennard River Station were both convenient and transitory. An immeasurably greater attraction was the secret life of the Bunuba male world. Admission to this world of ritual and mythology, of sacred sites, and of a living law flowing from the land, is gained through complex ceremonies and a long, arduous education. The ascent to manhood is a time that an Aboriginal man finds his place in his society and in nature – when he touches the invisible things of the past, present and future. It is a time of profound discovery. The ceremonial rites of the journey to manhood, carrying with it enormous responsibility and privilege, include instruction in social and moral law. There is also the opportunity to marry and to attend councils of lawmen. Importantly, admission to the law brings an intense obligation to family members.

Jandamarra's elevation to manhood was indeed profound. From this awareness and responsibility grew an intense emotional bond with his spirit country, Jumburr. The country of his father and grandfather, which he had come to know so well through the eyes of childhood innocence, took on far richer significance. Places he had been forbidden to see or go near because of some unfathomable threat of danger, were now accessible. These places, some of which contained the most intricate of paintings and sacred objects, told of the creation of his country and helped explain the invisible secret world.

Above the ceremonial ground where Jandamarra had undergone his initiation ceremony loomed the rock of the great Dreamtime hero, Dinkarra. To the south along the limestone range toward Baraa, the area was enriched by the most secret and fearsome male law. As Jandamarra's understanding of the complex spiritual world of his Bunuba inheritance grew, so too did his commitment to protect and defend his ancestral homeland. There was now no reason to return to Lukin's station and the country of his mother.

The most powerful influence during this period of intense education and rapid personal growth was Ellemarra. This man held a position of revered eminence in the Bunuba community. Although he had not reached the age where he was a custodian of all knowledge and wisdom, he was still a formidable lawman. His superb hunting skills, powerful personality and physical strength earned him widespread praise. At the time of Jandamarra's initiation, some three years had passed since Ellemarra's clever escape from Roebourne. That escape, and Ellemarra's subsequent belittling of the police and settlers who attempted to capture him, enhanced his already awesome status. Uncompromising and contemptuous of the settlers, he led frequent stock-killing raids on both Lillimooloora and Lennard River stations. To an impressionable Bunuba lad, Ellemarra was a person to emulate.

Jandamarra soon joined the stock-killing raids. What he did not realise was that Lukin had already laid charges of stealing sheep against him, simply because he had absconded. In late 1889, the young man encountered police troopers Armitage and Watts and two black troopers not far from Bandilngan. He knew the troopers and made no attempt to evade them. The police pretended to be friendly and persuaded Jandamarra to lead them to a concealed Bunuba encampment. The camp was stormed and Ellemarra and Packer, along with two others, were captured. The prisoners were chained by the neck and forced to walk the eighty-odd miles to Derby. Jandamarra was joined to the chain-gang.

Inspector Lodge, who had long considered Armitage the most efficient officer under his command, telegraphed Commissioner Phillips in Perth, reporting Ellemarra a captive again. He said it was a significant event, which would restore good relations between settlers and police. The settlers were delighted, believing this prized capture would significantly lessen sheep-killing.

All prisoners except Ellemarra were sentenced to six months in Derby prison. Ellemarra was given one year, plus an extra month at Roebourne to complete his previous unfinished term. Derby prison was a large, galvanised iron shed with a central post to which prisoners were chained at night. There was little ventilation. Even Derby residents complained of the pungent stench of the building. Prisoners spoke a variety of languages and some were traditionally hostile to others. They were all thrown together into the cesspit. Women too were often imprisoned in chains, simply to testify in court against males of their own family.

During the day, the chained prisoners worked in gangs, constructing and maintaining three miles of tram-track connecting the port with Derby's sparsely scattered population. Bishop Gibney, head of the Catholic Church in Western Australia, visited Derby in the early 1890s and described the sufferings of prisoners:

> *They are kept in irons, day and night, and work under a tropical sun in blistering heat on the roads, chained to the neck, one to another and also by the leg.*[1]

Despite the chains, escapes were common. By the early 1890s, it was impossible for the Derby gaoler to guard a prison population numbering up to ninety. Most got away by breaking the links with axes and picks. They were assisted by one fortunate legal ruling – the gaoler was prohibited from firing on escapees, a restriction that infuriated police and settlers.

A harsher, older statute of the convict era was the means of much more vindictive treatment of recaptured escapees. Police Magistrate Lodge regularly ordered up to fifty lashes. One Bunuba escapee, Mandingarry, was recaptured within sight of the safety of the Balili ranges, hauled back to Derby and flogged till he died. Lodge had commented, as if in justification, that those who managed to reach the safety of the limestone range became so determined that 'recapture was almost impossible'. There, he added, they became 'determined and vengeful'.[2]

Jandamarra was spared the harsher penalties of prison because the police recognised his skills as a horseman and drafted him into their service. For a period of almost two years, Jandamarra lived in the police stables where each day he fed, watered and exercised the police contingent of about twenty horses.

During his stay in Derby, he became well-known and popular among the white residents. The police used Jandamarra as a mascot and entered him in the occasional sports contest. He was a stylish boxer and never beaten in any of the hundred-yard foot-races he contested. On one occasion, he used his superb horse-riding skills with cutting humour at the expense of a local Kimberley identity. Matt O'Connell had left his much admired stallion, Whiteface, in the care of the Derby police while he was contracted to build the road from Derby to Halls Creek. An acclaimed bushman and explorer, he had boasted loudly that nobody but he could ride the great stallion. O'Connell returned to Derby to see Jandamarra riding Whiteface down the main street toward him, much to the amusement of the Derby onlookers. With a wry grin, Jandamarra delivered the horse to O'Connell. It was an act probably done casually, but it implied mockery nonetheless. Jandamarra had declared himself a social equal.

At the onset of the Wet season in 1891, Jandamarra returned to Bunuba country, having been separated from his homeland at a critical time in his life. His Derby sojourn had interrupted an important stage of manhood development. Normally a young man completing formal initiation would pass a long time in quiet reflection, often spanning several months and sometimes years, before finally coming to understand the spiritual richness of the world about him. Settlers and police had denied Jandamarra the chance to grow and merge fully into the spiritual richness of his country. He was seen by his elders as an incomplete initiate of the law that flowed from his ancestral lands.

From this point it appears that Jandamarra became a solitary figure, alienated from his peers by the inadequacy of his Bunuba education. Compared to others, he had suffered little at the hands of the invaders and seemed not to share the growing hatred of them.

The hardening of the Bunuba attitude and the absolute position of the settlers meant that an escalation of the conflict was inevitable. In July 1892, near Gunbi, Bunuba spearmen attacked a party of three gold prospectors. The lone survivor struggled to Lillimooloora Station with multiple spear wounds. Ironically, one of those killed was none other than Robert Allen, the same person who had assisted in Ellemarra's escape from Roebourne six years earlier. The attack was well planned, with Packer, a recently escaped Derby convict, luring the prospectors into an ambush at nightfall.

West Kimberley settlers reacted with unprecedented outrage. Their anger was voiced by the regular Derby correspondent to the *West Australian*. Supporting demands for a blood-letting revenge, he warned the government to issue no warrants 'but an abundance of ammunition'.[3] The same correspondent, writing in another newspaper, the *North West Times*, said he 'would not be surprised if the whole district turned out and avenged the murders in good old Queensland style'.[4]

The killings brought to the surface the settlers' fears of the Aboriginal people's ability to strike effectively against them. Their anxiety was acute. This attack appeared to have been led by a so-called 'semi-civilised' Aboriginal man. This was the essence of the fear. The whites thought that extensive contact with settlers made Aboriginal people dangerous once they returned to their homelands. Their view was that, having gained European skills, such people could influence and direct their more traditional countrymen.

Armitage led seven heavily armed troopers, four of them Aboriginal, to exact revenge. Six Bunuba women, captured and tortured, revealed the location of Packer's camp. The police, in a swift and ruthless attack, killed six Bunuba men including Packer, according to Armitage's journal. No prisoners were taken. Memories of the Jenulla affair three years earlier prompted Armitage to justify each fatality. 'They defied us,' he claimed and boasted, 'they had killed the white man and intended to kill us.'⁵ Bunuba people today say the official toll reflects a fraction of the number of people killed. Their story is that the police party indiscriminately shot down men, women and children in huge numbers. According to Banjo Woorunmurra, the police charged the camps, shooting everybody they could. Small children and babies were grabbed by their legs and had their heads smashed against the trunks of trees. This story is similar to other Bunuba accounts of frontier massacres.

The Bunuba were devastated by the Gunbi carnage. With glib satisfaction the police noted the 'salutary effect' of Armitage's punitive expedition. Ellemarra, the once vital mediator at the time of first contact, emerged once again to forge a peace between the Bunuba and police. Weeks after the killings, he enlisted as a black trooper under Armitage's command. This was neither surrender or betrayal but an ingenious attempt to safeguard lives.

Charming and persuasive, Ellemarra negotiated with Armitage certain conditions for his service. It was a de facto peace treaty. Bunuba people would be left unmolested by the police in return for a cessation of hostilities against the settlers of Lennard River and Lillimooloora stations.

Occasionally, police patrolled Bunuba country but, while Ellemarra escorted them, not one violent incident was recorded. The Armitage-Ellemarra partnership lasted eight months, during which time the Bunuba enjoyed peace without threat of police or settler attacks. For much of this time the Lennard River police unit operated against the Warrwa people at Oobagooma Station, the new West Kimberley flashpoint of frontier conflict.

In early 1893, such was the extent of the Warrwa attacks on the station, the police at Robinson River could no longer cope. Armitage, his new colleague, Goodridge, and Ellemarra were despatched twice to Oobagooma to crush the black warriors. In one desperate encounter Armitage, speared through the shoulder, wilted in front of Warrwa warriors moving in for the kill. Ellemarra forced them back courageously and was later almost single-handedly responsible for capturing nine of them. Armitage charged them with the murders of a settler and a Chinese cook, who had been speared several years earlier.

The wounded Armitage led the prisoners to Derby in triumph. It was his crowning glory, but owed to the man who was once the most feared Aboriginal warrior in the West Kimberley.

Armitage was soon promoted to sergeant and sent to the East Kimberley to quell the repeated Aboriginal attacks on the Halls Creek to Wyndham telegraph line. From there he pleaded for the Derby police to send him Ellemarra. 'No native assistant can replace him,' claimed Armitage desperately.[6] Despite a wide-ranging search, Ellemarra could not be found. The peace pact was uniquely forged through an arrangement between two individuals. With Armitage gone, Ellemarra's association with the police was no longer necessary.

During this period, Jandamarra stayed mostly around the Lillimooloora homestead. Here he witnessed and participated in the deterioration of Bunuba society. It was a traumatised society, with many Bunuba women, who sought station protection, having little choice but to accept sex with pastoral managers, stockmen and police officers. Sex was a central feature of frontier contact. Resident Magistrate Lovegrove observed in 1889 that many young women were kept around the Limalurru homestead for 'immoral purposes'. This, he said, was the major cause of Bunuba hostility.

For the sake of avoiding conflict, sexual liaison between young Bunuba women and the invaders was often sanctioned by old Bunuba people. There was also a pervading settler tolerance of sexual liaison with Aboriginal women but discretion was an unwritten frontier law. In 1893 Martin, the manager of Lillimooloora, received a stern censure from the West Kimberley settler community for blatantly maintaining a 'harem' of Bunuba women. Armitage was renowned for his violent sexual abuse of Aboriginal women and was once formally charged with rape. Yet, not surprisingly, the case never surfaced in court because the police refused to prosecute in spite of supporting evidence.

It was not only the settlers' libido that was flaunted at Lennard River and Lillimooloora stations. Jandamarra, who did not appreciate fully his manhood obligations, took advantage of the social chaos inflicted on his people. His sexual promiscuity became legendary. Attractive and charismatic, he drew young women toward him with ease. These vulnerable women, without husbands or fathers to protect them, probably looked to Jandamarra for security.

Jandamarra's sexual activities broke Bunuba law, as many of his girlfriends were in the wrong kinship group for him. Kinship law is basic to Aboriginal society. The pre-ordained skin name relates the individual to the family group and to the wider world. Breaking the strict kinship rules can have serious consequences. Punishment can occur in strange and unexpected ways. Through the powers of the spirit many relatives of the erring couple are also placed at risk.

Jandamarra's flagrant abuse of kinship rules highlighted the corruption and demise of traditional Bunuba authority. However, he did not escape unpunished; the lawmen banished him from mainstream Bunuba life. Now, Jandamarra had no choice but to live almost permanently at Lillimooloora and associate much more with the whites. He formed a close friendship with one particular settler whose name was Bill Richardson.

Richardson came to the Kimberley in early 1886 as a hopeful digger on the Halls Creek fields. Like most, he found little or no gold in the dry, stony creek beds. Rather than join the embittered throng retreating southward, Richardson stayed in the Kimberley and worked as a boundary rider on Lillimooloora Station. A solitary man, he was suited to remote station life.

In July 1892, just as Armitage and his party rode out on their killing spree at Gunbi, Richardson married Mary O'Connell, Derby's only single white woman. It is difficult to imagine a greater marital mismatch. She was a raucous woman, a drunk. He was reflective and sober, a rarity on the Kimberley frontier.

The night before his wedding, Richardson shared billy tea at a camp fire with a man named Gunning, a telegraph maintenance boss. Richardson was depressed and Gunning noted in his diary, 'Poor bastard, his [sic] marrying a real tartar.'[7] This solitary man soon discovered what most Derby residents already knew. His wife continued to sleep with several men around town. The couple separated and Mary was eventually transported to Fremantle Women's Industrial Institution for habitual drunkenness.

Richardson returned to his solitude at Lillimooloora, no doubt possessed by shame and embarrassment. There a rare and special friendship grew between two men from opposing cultures. Both were excluded from their respective societies. Richardson had gone to live at the end of the colonised world. There he felt he could escape from the harsh and hypocritical judgement of the community in Derby. On the other side of the Balili range lay the world of the Bunuba. Jandamarra was banished from that world to the land between. Richardson had nowhere else to go. The exile for one of them was only temporary. When occasion called, Jandamarra would be drawn back and welcomed by his people.

STATE OF SIEGE

IN LATE 1893, THE COLONIAL world tightened its grip on the Bunuba. For the first time, settlers moved large herds of cattle to the border country. The Bunuba had learned to manage sheep but cattle were a frightening prospect. They resisted the awesome beasts by chasing them away from important places, and often speared them. The settlers felt more and more threatened. With the white population in decline as many deserted the Kimberley for the Coolgardie goldfields, there was a heightened state of vulnerability for those who remained. Both the Bunuba and the settlers began to feel under siege: a potent situation that foreshadowed unprecedented mass killings of the traditional owners.

The Bunuba had begun the year victoriously. Armitage was not replaced, leaving only the incompetent bushman Goodridge to head the Lennard River police camp. The decision to have just one police constable with two black troopers reflected the declining economic worth of the area. Ten years had passed since Lukin and Forrester were seen as the most fortunate of all Kimberley pastoralists. Now the area where they had placed their runs drifted toward economic ruin. In July 1893, to cap a decade of opposition from the Bunuba, Lillimooloora was auctioned.

For propaganda purposes the settlers put out word that the station had been sold because of the sheep spearers. The real reason was that James Munro's greed propelled him to bankruptcy after the Melbourne land-crash of the early 1890s, forcing him to sell all his assets. The once acclaimed station was no longer an economic proposition. Ongoing Bunuba raids and low wool prices saw to that. With no bids, the station was passed in and came under the control of the Union Bank. Martin continued as manager but, without money to build up the flocks and build and repair fences, he was really just a caretaker.

The Kimberley economy was depressed, reeling from two years of drought and low wool prices. Ten years earlier, the region had been seen as the state's economic saviour. It was now a parasite on the colony's finances, with significant sums of public money being needed to prop up European occupation. Steamships, the lifeblood of the Kimberley settlement, depended on government subsidies. There were two highly paid resident magistrates, a host of public servants and various public works all financed from government coffers. The police contingent in the Kimberley was greater than the Perth and Fremantle police forces combined. 'Remove the staff of government officials,' claimed the *West Australian*, cynically, 'and the [settler] population would only be a handful.' It went on to warn, 'The Kimberley cannot remain as it is or a demand for its abandonment must arise.'[1]

The Kimberley settlement was saved by the discovery of gold at Coolgardie in 1892. The subsequent gold rush doubled Western Australia's settler population to a hundred thousand within three years. Although the rush was far to the south, the booming population needed beef and the Kimberley had already shown its capacity to graze cattle.

With shrewd business acumen Isadore Emanuel quickly seized the opportunity. He stocked his Upper Fitzroy runs with herds of imported cattle and these became the foundation of the West Kimberley beef expansion. But Emanuel was not the first pastoralist to graze cattle on the west side. His friends, William and Charles McDonald, had overlanded cattle in 1885 to establish Fossil Downs Station. For years the McDonald brothers survived on credit from Derby merchants until the southern population boom gave them real profits. These pioneers proved that cattle could thrive in the fertile but rocky range country. The Bunuba domain, uninviting for sheep, was now seen as ideal cattle country.

A few miles north of the place where travellers forded Bandaral ngarri, later known as Fitzroy Crossing, Joe Blythe established Gurangadja Station in 1893. Bordering the southern Bunuba fort-ress-wall of Ganimbiri – a continuation of the Balili plateau – it was rich country. Bandaral ngarri, Brooking Creek and countless springs provided abundant water for ever-increasing numbers of cattle. Importantly, a little way from Blythe's homestead, a strategic gap in Ganimbiri offered a gateway to the fertile cattle country north-ward. At Gurangadja, Blythe would be in the forefront of the major confrontation with Bunuba people.

Joe Blythe was born in the small south-west town of Bunbury in 1847. It was also the birthplace of John and Alexander Forrest. Blythe and the Forrest brothers shared their formative youth until their life-paths diverged. The Forrest boys enjoyed the social privilege of a Hale school education in Perth and later cemented their associ-ation with colonial gentry by marrying into the aristocratic families, the Hamersleys and the Barrett-Lennards. John became Western Australia's first Premier while Alexander played second fiddle as the inaugural Kimberley parliamentary representative and Lord Mayor of Perth. Blythe, in contrast, had a rudimentary education and was described as 'semi-literate' in adult life.

Blythe was possessed by a demonic will to succeed. His father was one of the perpetrators of the bloodbath at Pinjarra in 1834. He and the other killers under Stirling's command handed down the story to their children, who grew up in conquered Nyoongar lands, painting the massacre as the celebrated 'Battle of Pinjarra'. This myth helped shape Blythe's belief in the righteousness of the fight to take the lands of Aboriginal people, even if it meant their slaughter.

The marriage to his childhood sweetheart Mary Coppin produced eight children in eleven years. The family struggled in poverty, running a small dairy farm near the south-west town of Nannup until a disease wiped out the cows. Financially ruined, and grieving over the death of his only daughter, Blythe took the family to Derby in 1884. He was driven by these past hardships and determined to create an economic future for his sons in the Kimberley.

Blythe detested the smell of alcohol and cruelly punished any of his sons whom he caught drinking, but saw it as a way to make easy money. He opened the first hotel in Derby, the Victoria, which settler John Collins described as nothing but a grog shop. Soon Blythe had competition from two more hotels, catering for the crazed drinking of frontier settlers. The occurrence books of the Derby police give lucid descriptions of the pervading alcohol abuse, with daily repetition. Drinking shaped the culture, affecting most settlers, regardless of their economic or social position.

Stock Inspector Morrison, who occasionally relieved the resident magistrate, was often so intoxicated he could not write official reports. Police officers themselves were regularly drunk on duty, and there were frequent dismissals. Even the Derby gaoler boozed regularly while in charge of chained prisoners. From this drunken misery Blythe made quick money and invested in other businesses with his elder sons, Charlie, Joe Jr and Arthur. He purchased horses, camels and wagons and carted wool and other items between pastoral stations and Derby.

Blythe decided that Derby, described by one visitor as 'a hell hole', was not the place to bring up adolescent children. In 1889, after his teenage sons Lindsay and Roland were charged with petty theft, he accepted Emanuel's offer to manage Noonkanbah Station. Blythe soon earned the reputation of a hard-nosed manager who treated Aboriginal workers as slaves. Banjo Woorunmurra, who grew up on Blythe family stations, recalls the old people describing Blythe as a heartless and cruel man. A common means by which he attempted to create a terrified and servile Aboriginal station workforce was to 'heel' those he captured escaping the work teams, by cutting their achilles tendons.

Even his sons had to be 'near dead' to be excused from work. This, his family memoirs say, led to family tragedy in August 1893. Dismissing the complaints of fever from sixteen-year-old Lindsay, Blythe ordered him to muster horses on a distant paddock. Two days later Lindsay was found dead from thirst.

To this day, Aboriginal people say that young Blythe died foolishly. He became lost looking for a well-known waterhole. His horse had broken down and in the searing heat the dying boy wrote a farewell note to his family. An Aboriginal man found the body and took the scribbled message to Joe Blythe. His father was stricken with grief and later rejected a finding of accidental death by a coronial inquiry. Blythe knew the lad had been found close to water and was a good bushman. Legend has it that old Blythe understood and feared the power of Aboriginal magic and blamed the old lawmen for singing his son to death. Increasingly, he became obsessed with the idea of bloody retribution against the alleged perpetrators. Yet his chance for revenge would not occur for almost a year and a half.

The opportunity for Blythe's blood-letting would come about after a rise in his social position thrust him into direct confrontation with the Bunuba. His transition from Noonkanbah manager to Gurangadja grazier would not have occurred without Isadore Emanuel's backing. Emanuel supplied Blythe with cattle on long-term credit. In a way,

Blythe acted as an agent for a mighty alliance between Emanuel and Alexander Forrest. In mid-1894, Isadore and Alexander formalised their association, naming it Emanuel, Forrest and Company.

Any economic union that included Alexander Forrest was bound to be powerful. This Kimberley colonial founding father had well-entrenched political and business connections. His credentials were impressive; apart from his membership of parliament, the northern landholder was the largest stock and land agent in Western Australia. He was also purported to be the colony's richest man, after profiting handsomely from the frenzy of the stock exchange speculation which accompanied the gold rush.

Flush with cash, Alexander bought up the West Kimberley stations of Oobagooma, Meda and Gilgurry, and also acquired a part-stake in prestigious Liveringa. In early 1894, he purchased Plum Plain from Sydney businessman Jack Plum and renamed it Jubilee Downs. This flood-prone flat land was the southernmost portion of Bunuba country.

On the surface, Alexander Forrest was the dominant partner. Despite Emanuel's large Kimberley holdings and his prominence as a political lobbyist, he was not a member of Western Australia's colonial elite. Not quite thirty, Emanuel kept his Jewish patriarchal and financial headquarters in New South Wales. Yet it seems Emanuel was the dynamic force of the partnership. One informed observer described him as 'hard as a nail in a deal, shrewd in gauging chances', and spoke of the 'genius' of Emanuel, Forrest and Company[2]. There is no question as to who benefited most. While Forrest lodged his West Kimberley stations under the new company name, Emanuel retained his holdings totally in his family's corporate structure.

By 1894, Forrest and Emanuel had a stranglehold on the region's beef-producing land and moved to control the shipping trade as well. They booked all available space for livestock on the coastal steamers and then became the official agents for the Adelaide Steamship Company, the major shipping line on the west coast. Emanuel and Forrest's domination of the West Kimberley cattle industry was enhanced when they recruited the McDonald brothers and Meeda Station manager Felix Edgar as cattle buyers.

To corner the goldfields beef market and beat competition from the Duracks, who were rapidly amassing cattle in the East Kimberley, Forrest and Emanuel needed to build up their cattle herds urgently. For this they demanded new pastures on lands still in the control of Aboriginal people. The West Kimberley landscape drew the cattle relentlessly toward the ranges. The sheep growers occupying the vast grassy plains didn't understand the beef industry and kept cattle out for decades to come. South of the Fitzroy lay endless desert sands. Those with a vision of roaming cattle-herds looked to the fertile country beyond the limestone rampart. But this was country of the Bunuba, who had signalled that invasion would not go unchallenged.

They stood between a half-crazed Joe Blythe and his dream to create a pastoral empire for himself and his heirs. As far as Emanuel was concerned, there was no more determined front-man to take on and defeat these menacing Aborigines, who dared to hold up the advance of civilisation.

The Bunuba had become familiar with those cattle that provided beef to the settlers on Lennard River and Lillimooloora stations. Seeing them as fierce, the people dubbed them Maranggangarri, a name derived from their devil-like horns. But at this time they were few in number. The odd wandering horned beast was either killed or chased away from zealously guarded sacred areas and waterholes.

This situation changed dramatically when Blythe brought in large herds of cattle. Intrusive and destructive, a few of these massive creatures would totally ruin a waterhole. The Bunuba knew also that with cattle would come the settler and his gun. By the beginning of

1894, the Bunuba felt besieged more than at any other time during the ten-year period of conflict with whites.

Blythe was heartened by the good soaking rains that fell just before Christmas 1893. The few showers during the previous wet season had hardly dampened the scorched earth. These heavy rains continued intermittently until early February 1894. As the settlers celebrated the breaking of the drought, storm clouds gathered over the Leopold Range plateau. For twenty-four hours, a ceaseless barrage of water deluged an area that fed the Bandaral ngarri, Mayalnga and Lennard rivers.

The gently flowing Bandaral ngarri was transformed into a violent torrent. Fossil Downs homestead was submerged and most of the McDonalds' cattle were washed away. Blythe's homestead, doubling as the Fitzroy Crossing hotel and store, was obliterated by the advancing water. He and sons Charlie, Joe and Arthur survived by clinging to tree-tops for three days. The telegraph operator stationed ten miles away on what was thought to be safe high ground, spent the same period marooned on the roof of his stone building. He reported later the incredible sight of a sea of muddy water stretching to all horizons.

While lightning and thunder from the cyclonic clouds had given some notice of the impending Bandaral ngarri flood, the settlers on the Lennard received no warning of what was about to befall them. At the Bandilngan entrance, Martin was mustering sheep into the yards when suddenly the earth shuddered with a thundering noise. At first he presumed it was an earthquake, then recoiled in horror at the sight of a one-hundred-foot high wall of water tearing through the gorge. As the deafening roar approached, Martin and his workers clambered frantically up the Napier cliff-face, away from the gorge. They watched the swirling brown waters sweep all before them, including many of Lillimooloora's sheep and fences. Boab trees, hundreds of years old, were uprooted like fragile bushes and carried toward the ocean.

The maelstrom of water engulfed the Lennard River flat lands, creating a murky sea, stretching for miles. Fourteen thousand of Lukin's sheep perished and most of his fencing disappeared. Overall, the great 1894 flood destroyed thirty thousand sheep, several hundred cattle and hundreds of miles of fencing. The unexpected torrent flooded the Aboriginal camp at Alf Barnett's Balmangara Station (later to become Kimberley Downs), drowning many of the old people, who had no chance of escape. The police reported old Aboriginal people saying that never had they experienced such a surge of water. At one point the waters of the Bandaral ngarri and Lennard converged to form an inland sea a hundred miles wide, a phenomenon never repeated since.

The flood was the death-knell for Lillimooloora. Soon afterwards the station was broken up and incorporated into adjacent holdings. Lukin's vision of pastoral grandeur lay dissolved amidst the mud and the stench of rotting sheep carcasses. A pleasant surprise for the Bunuba was the destruction of the police station at Lennard River but soon, to their disappointment, troopers took up residence at the deserted Lillimooloora homestead.

Officially, the flood was explained by coastal cyclonic activity, which had caused a massive rain-bearing depression to open up over the Milawundi range. But the Bunuba, no doubt, saw the work of mysterious and magical forces. Those young men who may have thought the ancient laws lacked power in the new, settler-imposed order, saw the strength of their cultural traditions. Now, the settlers faced a resurgent Bunuba spirit.

Emphasising the serious state of affairs, the Derby correspondent to the *West Australian* announced: 'Every boat that sails from Derby takes more of our residents away.'[3] Already hurt financially by the wool recession, many were ruined now by the flood. It wasn't just the landholders who were affected; many white workers would not tolerate decreased wages and left the Kimberley for the Kalgoorlie goldfields.

One of those seen leaving was William Lukin. He cut a depressing figure as he ascended the gangway of the ship at the Derby wharf. As one of the few remaining original settlers and a vocal advocate of local interests, his departure was a symbolic blow to community morale. But Lukin had not abandoned the district. Confused and depressed, he simply retreated south to ponder his future. Two months later he returned, vowing not to concede defeat to the Bunuba or the power of nature embodied in the Kimberley lands.

The Bunuba could claim victory on the Lennard country but the situation was different on their southern border, where Blythe treated the flood as a temporary setback. With his sons he constructed a new Gurangadja homestead (near where the homestead stands today), close to the Ganimbiri wall. Not only did he recover his cattle losses but he increased his herd significantly. He was supported by Emanuel, who survived the flood almost unscathed.

As Blythe prepared to move cattle north of Ganimbiri, the stage was set for an historic confrontation. In a letter to the *West Australian*, Blythe claimed that the Aborigines had 'swarmed' down from the hills causing havoc with his cattle.[4] He was angered by a Bunuba strategy of chasing cattle away from waterholes.

With such skilful herd management, the Bunuba contained Blythe's cattle to a small patch of land between the Crossing and the junction of the Bandaral ngarri and Mayalnga rivers. In this situation the beasts could not be fattened. For as long as the Bunuba held the rocky highlands, the exasperated Blythe found it almost impossible to expand his pasture capacity. On the map he possessed a one-million-acre property, yet the Bunuba ensured that his cattle grazed only a fraction of it.

In frustration, Blythe publicly blamed the police, condemning a normal patrol of 'two inferior bushmen and a nondescript native assistant' as totally inadequate. 'To ask the police to come to our aid is absurd,' claimed Blythe bluntly. The Native Police system of Queensland was the solution, he urged, advising that the unit be 'of eight to ten lads each weighing about eight stone and under the command of a couple of whites'. He proposed the force be split in two, concluding, 'They would do more in six months than the present system could do in years.'⁵ His proposal was so similar to others put forward by settlers that one assumes the topic of the black police force was common conversation on the Kimberley frontier.

The Queensland Native Police Force system was nothing short of institutional genocide. Armed Aboriginal troopers, recruited from remote districts, were licensed to carry out indiscriminate slaughter of men, women and children. The frontier settlers of west and north Queensland accepted this murderous system as the solution to 'their Aboriginal problem'. But those in Western Australian Government authority had for a long time cited the bloodstained Queensland frontier as an example to be avoided.

Never in Western Australian colonial history had settlers confronted such strong Aboriginal resistance as that facing them now in the Kimberley mountains. The Queensland influence on Kimberley colonisation was no doubt a factor contributing to the virulent advocacy of a black police force. This was particularly evident in the East Kimberley where the Duracks, economic beneficiaries of the native police in Queensland, were persistent advocates for the introduction of a similar system. However, Police Commissioner Phillips dismissed Michael Durack's call for native police as 'objectionable', arguing that the police could not be used to kill British subjects indiscriminately.

This official objection did not stop men of political influence demanding bloodshed. Francis Connor, the inaugural parliamentary member for East Kimberley, vigorously took up the call for the introduction of a Native Police Force. In October 1893, he moved in the Western Australian Legislative Assembly:

> . . . that in view of the danger and loss being caused in the Kimberley through the action of the blacks it is necessary to have established a force of native troopers and trackers, for the protection of the settlers and their property in those districts . . . I ask whether the natives are to have this country or the whites?[6]

Not to be outdone, Alexander Forrest proposed that a contingent of black troopers be sent to operate against the West Kimberley hill tribes who 'drive the settlers' sheep and cattle to the hills, and simply laugh at their pursuers'. With his sights set on the Bunuba, Forrest concluded, 'I ask whether the life of one European is not worth a thousand natives as far as the settlement of this country is concerned?'[7]

John Forrest, who was knighted soon after he became Western Australia's first premier, pleaded successfully for the motion to be withdrawn. He argued that, while having 'the greatest sympathy' for the Kimberley settlers, he was not in a position to 'sanction anything that will lead to the impression that an indiscriminate slaughter of blackfellows will be tolerated or allowed by the Government of the colony'.[8] The Premier was referring to the delicate political relationship with the British Government over the treatment of Aboriginal people in Western Australia.

The British Government did not trust the incoming Forrest government to protect the lives of Aboriginal people as British subjects. In 1890 the British gave restricted political independence to Western Australian colonists and, through S70 of the 1889 Western Australian Constitution Act, its Perth-based Governor retained responsibility for Aboriginal people's protection and welfare. The legislation also established the Aboriginal Protection Board, to enable the Governor to meet his legal responsibilities. Despite the fact that the Board could operate effectively only through the cooperation of Western Australian Government agencies, such as the police force and the judiciary, its independence was a threat to many colonists. Their concerns were put in a graphic way by Septimus Burt, representing northern pastoral interests in the legislature:

> if there is any attempt by this Board to interfere with the present rela-
> tionship between blacks and whites in the north . . . there will be war
> and the Aboriginal Protection Board will be swept away.[9]

As soon as ink was dry on the Constitution Act the Forrest Government campaigned to bring the Aboriginal Protection Board under its control and to stop the British Government from having direct responsibility for Aboriginal affairs. It continued to do this through persistently arguing with the British Government that Section 70 was inconsistent with self-government, and that the independent colonial government was capable of protecting Aboriginal people and administering their welfare in the British tradition of 'justice and fairness'. Official violence against Kimberley Aborigines jeopardised the delicate political negotiations being conducted by Sir John Forrest.

Kimberley settlers felt deserted and betrayed by a government which they believed should have been more supportive of them. The gerrymandered Western Australian Parliament, independent since 1890 and dominated by members representing northern pastoral communities, had in fact shown greater sympathy to the northern settlers at the expense of Aboriginal people, who faced yet more oppression. Amendments to the Aboriginal Offenders Act and Aboriginal Protection Act in 1892 and 1893 increased prison penalties for both stock-killing and absconding from contract labour, and reintroduced whipping as a punishment. Also, by appointing prominent settlers as JPs, the government empowered the pastoral community with the legal means to treat Aboriginal people even more harshly.

The West Kimberley district was favoured by this system of government patronage. Within two years of political independence, settlers Isadore Emanuel, William Lukin, William McLarty, George Rose and Charles McDonald were appointed as justices. They had the power to sentence Aboriginal people to prison for three years, order a flogging of up to fifty lashes and validate two-year work contracts with bonded black servants. They could also issue to police officers warrants of arrest. No longer did the resident magistrate in Derby have a monopoly of judicial power. The police now were very much in the hands of the West Kimberley squatters.

Yet these powers were not enough to defeat the determined Bunuba, who had accumulated ten years of resistance experience. Their vigorous opposition held up the Blythe vanguard from pushing cattle into the hilly Kimberley interior. After reported stock killings near Fitzroy Crossing in March 1894, the Derby correspondent to the *North West Times* summed up both the settlers' frustrations and the tricky political situation by suggesting:

> Now that Exeter Hall has got her hands and ears full, listening to the cries about the supposed ill usage of conquered tribes in South Africa . . . It would be a good time for the Western Australian Government to shut its eyes for say three months and let the settlers up here have a little time to teach the nigger the difference between mine and thine . . . it would only have to be done once, and once done, could easily be forgotten.[10]

At the time, it was meant to be a political statement to pressure the government to act decisively against the Bunuba and other resistant Kimberley Aboriginal groups but, as later events unfolded, it turned out to be a horrific prophecy. Again settlers demanded that police act independently of Perth headquarters. 'Discretionary power' for the district's police chief was still the popular catchcry, in reality a call for the police to have freedom to shoot Aboriginal people with impunity. However, the demands were rejected by Government on the traditional lines that this would lead to uncontrolled bloodshed.

In frustration, West Kimberley settlers vented their anger on the local Parliamentary member. To many there appeared little benefit in having the Premier's brother as their representative. Increasingly, there was the view that Alexander Forrest was too involved in business dealings in the south to be worried about his Kimberley constituents. He had visited the district twice only, the first as an explorer in 1879 and then four years later, with his brother, to buy land.

His absence from the area was noted with contempt by many. It was widely held that Isadore Emanuel would have defeated Forrest convincingly had he contested the 1894 election. Despite repeated requests Emanuel declined to stand, stating that he would not run against his friend. Little did settlers realise that during the run up to the election, Emanuel and Forrest were conspiring to carve up the West Kimberley for themselves.

Forrest had previously been elected unopposed, but this time he faced a stern challenge from a Broome pearler named Streeter. Although Forrest won the election, fifty-nine votes to twenty-eight, it was said that had more pearlers enrolled Forrest would have lost. The election challenge motivated Forrest to visit his electorate in July 1894.

At a well-attended meeting in a Derby hotel, Forrest was introduced to the crowd by Emanuel, who sought an answer to a question on Aborigines. Forrest responded and to the applause of the crowd stated that he believed, 'competent inspectors isolated from Perth should largely have discretionary powers'.[11] He would raise the matter with his brother in Perth.

One 'competent' man to whom Forrest alluded was Sub-inspector Overand Drewry. Not long afterwards, Drewry was given the much talked-about 'discretionary powers'. These were to lead to an unprecedented slaughter of hundreds of Aboriginal people throughout the West Kimberley.

REBELLION

THE RISE OF OVERAND DREWRY to sub-inspector was meteoric. On arrival in Western Australia in 1892, he joined the police force as sergeant. His curriculum vitae looked impressive to the head of the Western Australian Police Force. British born, he was twenty-eight, extremely fit, an experienced horseman who had spent four years with the Canadian Mounted Police, much of it in combat with Indigenous people in north-west Canada. Within months he was posted to the Kimberley, where he took over from Lodge as head of police.

Frustrated by constraints on police operations, Drewry united with the settlers to demand discretionary powers and squads of black troopers. The government refused to act but did relax restrictions when a white trooper named Collins was speared in July 1893 as he led an assault on an encampment near Durack and Kilfoyle's Rosewood stations, south-east of Wyndham. Though he paid for it with his life, Collins' murderous attack cost the lives of twenty-three Miriwoong people.

This 'pile of dead victims', as the *Catholic Record* put it, describing the event as a 'massacre', was not enough to satisfy the East Kimberley settlers.[1] They used Collins' death to demand a military campaign against the defiant Aborigines of the East Kimberley mountains. The government relented and changed the rules of police operations.

In October 1893, a heavily armed police expedition of four white and four black troopers left Wyndham. Led by Sergeant Brophy, the police were instructed to 'disperse' Aborigines along the Ord, Osmond and other rivers to avenge Collins' death. The word 'disperse' in Australian colonial language meant randomly shooting Aboriginal people with intent to terrorise and kill. Nobody suggested issuing warrants or taking prisoners. The party returned to Wyndham a month later and, by its own report, had killed a total of thirty Aboriginal people in numerous attacks. Nowhere in his report did Brophy connect any of the dead with Collins' killing. Brophy's body-count did not satisfy Drewry, whose report to Commissioner Phillips concluded with a frightening glimpse into future police operations:

They have got a lesson this time . . . that is really required to be applied twice annually for the next three years or so . . . They might then be taught to respect the lives and property of the whites . . . [2]

Soon afterwards, the Kimberley Police Force was divided and Drewry took charge of the western side. He was frustrated that no event occurred to prompt a similar campaign of terror against the Bunuba and was embarrassed by the incompetent officers under his command.

In the early 1890s, the Police Department sent most troopers with bush experience to the East Kimberley. That district's increased stock-spearing and attacks on the telegraph line in mountainous terrain required tougher troopers than those posted to the west. In the West Kimberley, officers with urban backgrounds, many of whom were recent English immigrants, became at times the butt of sarcastic settler humour. Blythe told Drewry that Aborigines of the Upper

Fitzroy bragged that police could capture only those who were 'old, blind and deaf'. One police officer, Clifton, in charge of the Fitzroy outpost on Noonkanbah Station, was admonished by Drewry 'not to bring in any other old men'.[3]

Drewry set out to transform his command and rid it of inefficient bushmen. He complained regularly to Commissioner Phillips about the calibre of his force. The Robinson River police camp was in disarray because Constable Child could not get along with Constable McGilvrey. When McGilvrey was transferred to the Lennard, Drewry reported sarcastically, 'He rode around the country everywhere except where the natives were.' It was alleged by Drewry that the discontented Goodridge 'wanted a transfer anywhere except the camp he is on'.[4]

When Clifton and Goodridge resigned in early 1894, Drewry warned he would not tolerate replacements from the south 'not worth their salt'.[5] Instead, he asked that the men be replaced by two Oobagooma stockmen, both good bushmen and fine horsemen. Phillips agreed but reminded Drewry that the recruits must understand 'that the Queensland way of dealing with natives does not apply here'.[6]

Yet it was an important precedent, for previous policy had been not to recruit locals as troopers, thus enabling the government to proclaim publicly that the Kimberley Police Force was independent of settlers. To give the appearance that there was no radical change in recruitment practice, Phillips ordered that the recruits undergo orientation in Perth. They refused and were not appointed.

Undeterred, Drewry considered recruiting other local bushmen to man police outposts. The Lennard River camp had become a sensitive issue because Lukin, having returned with renewed enthusiasm, agitated for the outpost to be strengthened. Drewry reasoned that one competent white trooper in command of two black troopers could manage since the Bunuba no longer threatened here as they had done before.

The ideal person to take charge of the Lennard camp was William Richardson, who was already doing the job in a de facto way. Drewry reported that, of the twenty Aborigines arrested since McGilvrey had been stationed at the Lennard, most had been captured by Richardson. With Jandamarra's support Richardson caught and interned Aboriginal people at the new Lillimooloora Police station or Lukin's homestead until the police came to collect them. Richardson had never thought much about becoming a policeman but the idea appealed because there was far more money to be made hunting Aboriginal people than doing station work.

Richardson and Oobagooma stockman Spong agreed to undergo basic police training in Perth. When they returned in May 1894, Spong was posted to the Fitzroy camp and, predictably, Richardson replaced McGilvrey, who was sacked.

These were the first Kimberley stockmen to join the police. Their bush skills and familiarity with the country advantaged police operations. Possibly of greater importance was their entrée into local Aboriginal communities and their ability to recruit loyal black troopers.

Black troopers were pivotal to police operations, particularly against recalcitrant Aboriginal groups in the hills with a decade of experience with settlers. The police, however, were dogged by disloyalty. It had long been recognised that many black troopers recruited from the south were frightened by local Aborigines. Frequent absconding had led to police immobility and chaos. On one occasion, an Aboriginal trooper named Peter absconded from a routine Robinson River patrol. It took three weeks to find the scattered horses and, even then, the police became hopelessly lost returning to Derby. Another well-known ploy was for black troopers to follow fresh footprints then branch off to follow old tracks leading inevitably to a deserted campsite.

Richardson brought with him Jandamarra, the expert marksman and horseman, a prized recruit with knowledge of the intricacies of the country and its inhabitants. No Bunuba had worked with the police since Ellemarra's association with Armitage. That arrangement benefited the Bunuba but Jandamarra's police alliance was different. The exile appeared to have no obligation to protect his people.

The settlers had no doubts. Jandamarra joined Richardson to form the most effective police unit the West Kimberley had seen. Strangely, Jandamarra was not recruited by the police – he simply rode on patrols in Richardson's private service. Officially, Richardson had been assigned only one black trooper, named Captain. Born at La Grange Bay south of the pearling town of Broome, thirty-five year-old Captain was drafted to the police via Rottnest Island Prison. His contact with settlers went back many years to the time when he was a pearl-diver and learnt to speak English well.

Appreciating Richardson's links to the Lennard area, Drewry counselled him not to become 'a private constable of Lukin'.[7] His orders were to spend as much time on other stations as he did on Lennard River. His patrols covered an enormous tract of country, spanning the area from the Meda River near Derby to Brooking Creek near Bandaral ngarri. It covered the pastoral properties of Balmangara, Lennard River, Lillimooloora, Ganimbiri and Gurangadja. With the exception of Balmangara, all the properties bordered Bunuba country.

No matter how efficient, Richardson's unit alone could not bring the Bunuba to heel. Drewry, the creative military commander, planned a two-pronged assault on the Bunuba bastion. Richardson would police the Balili plateau and part of Ganimbiri, and the Fitzroy troopers would strike where Blythe planned to graze his cattle.

In July 1894, Spong was reinforced at the Fitzroy by a man who so violently terrorised Aboriginal people that he is named today by their descendants as a mass murderer. Richard Pilmer, a New Zealander, migrated to Western Australia at the age of twenty-nine in 1890. After a failed stint on the Murchison goldfields, he joined the police force in Geraldton and, as he later described it, was soon despatched with orders 'to teach the wild Australian blackfellow the rights of property in the great unfenced'.[8]

In the Murchison and Gascoyne districts, Pilmer learned how to capture large numbers of Aborigines in the bush. Later, he would use the practice extensively in the Kimberley. In his autobiography, the technique is explained:

> When rushing a camp, if one of the natives got well away, you galloped after him, took him to the first tree or sapling, sat him down with his legs around it and handcuffed his ankles to secure him. You would then hop on your horse and continue rounding up the camp, put all you wanted on the chain, go back and gather up those that you may have hobbled round the tree.[9]

Pilmer's autobiography is a revealing document. He romanticises his father's days in the British Army in New Zealand during the Maori wars. His own undeclared war was with the Aboriginal people of northern Western Australia. After eighteen months in the Gascoyne, Pilmer applied for a transfer to the Kimberley. Life had become 'too humdrum' where he was. A combination of Rottnest Island prison cells, cat o' nine tails and the breaking of the drought had brought about the demise of the 'last of the black highway men' there. The Kimberley he saw was 'still a land of adventure and of the conflict of the white man with the black'.[10]

Pilmer and Spong were assigned two Bunuba prisoners from Derby prison, Lilamarra and Longaradale, and ordered to the Upper Fitzroy.

Here Emanuel was rapidly building up his herd and welcomed the police support. On the first patrol Pilmer's party amassed twenty-five prisoners. Never in the district's police operations had so many been chained on one patrol. The tally would have been higher had not Pilmer released the older men. The Mt Abbot police camp was transformed temporarily into a makeshift court, presided over by Isadore Emanuel JP. Every prisoner was sentenced to Derby prison for terms ranging from twelve months to two years, plus a flogging of twenty-five lashes.

Their next patrol produced an incident which rang alarm bells for police and settlers throughout the district. On a July night in 1894, after Emanuel had sentenced all eighteen prisoners, Pilmer awoke to the sounds of crunching metal. The sight of Longaradale and Lilamarra attempting to release the prisoners by cutting their chains with an axe, prompted Pilmer to open fire. Both mutineers fled taking with them a Winchester rifle and a Webley revolver. This was more than just black troopers absconding. It was unprecedented – attempted armed mutiny against police authority.

Images of armed and hostile Aboriginal people haunted nervous police and settlers. An earlier incident near the Robinson River in 1893 showed how the police panicked and resorted to violence when Aborigines captured firearms. When they found their temporarily abandoned outpost pillaged and a rifle and revolver missing, the police charged off. Days later, the troopers stormed the targeted Aboriginal camp at daybreak, killing eight, including two women and a child, as they awoke from sleep. The relieved troopers reported that the recovered guns had never been fired.

Soon after the attempted mutiny at Mt Abbot, Drewry ordered his men to accompany their armed black troopers at all times. But this instruction was impossible to carry out. Institutional police practice determined that armed black troopers were often out of a policeman's view. This occurred when police prepared to attack an encampment or when black troopers hunted food for police and prisoners.

Few black troopers displayed complete loyalty. Pilmer was bedevilled by rebellious Aboriginal police. He blamed Drewry for appointing Longaradale and Lilamarra and personally selected four more from Derby prison, two of whom escaped on their first patrol. In contrast, Richardson had complete trust in his black troopers. Jandamarra was his friend and Captain's traumatic memories of Rottnest Island's overcrowded prison cells directed him to ride with the police in unquestioning obedience.

Richardson's unit had immediate impact. Within days of taking up the police post, Ellemarra was captured. This great man once again walked behind a policeman's horse with a hot metal chain rattling around his neck. At Lennard River Station Lukin, now a Justice of the Peace, awaited revenge. The warrant cited Ellemarra's killing of two sheep, although Lukin wrote later that he could have pressed at least one thousand separate charges. He sentenced the brooding Ellemarra to three years and sent him to Derby, his back lacerated from a flogging by a rawhide whip. Perhaps disturbed by the treatment of his one-time hero, Jandamarra disappeared into the hills and waited for Richardson and Captain to return.

Derby had changed since Ellemarra had been imprisoned there in 1890. In mid-1894, Aboriginal prisoners outnumbered the remaining settlers of the dusty little town. There was also an Aboriginal fringe-camp edging onto the mudflats. Here, about fifty people lived in atrocious conditions, having long been forced off their traditional lands, barely surviving on limited welfare provisions from the Aboriginal Protection Board. Their plight aroused only antipathy from the local white community, with one Derby resident complaining that he could not sleep at night because of women wailing over the many children who died in the camp.

There was also a new and bigger prison, built a year earlier to cater for more prisoners. It was divided into two; the larger, open compound held the occasional Asian and European prisoners, while Aborigines were crammed into cells made of iron and brick, where they remained chained, day and night. They only felt direct sunlight when they walked, chained, with their pick axes to build the roads of Derby.

Ellemarra was soon joined by six Bunuba prisoners brought in by Richardson's patrol. These prisoners, no doubt, told the story of having attacked Richardson in their frantic bid to escape the chain. Fearlessly, Jandamarra had rushed to Richardson's rescue, saving his life and preventing any prisoners from escaping. Ellemarra may have been confused by the actions of his young countryman, but now the police had no reason to doubt Jandamarra's loyalty.

George Bell, the gaoler, saw Ellemarra as a model prisoner, a willing worker whose forceful leadership aided prison management. Ellemarra organised work teams and disciplined those who challenged prison authority. But the gaoler was unable to recognise or appreciate the spell cast by this witty and charming man on his companions.

Ellemarra waited patiently, then seized his opportunity to escape with masterly ease. It was mid-August 1894, and the prison, without whites or Asians, could not fulfil the wood-carting contract it had with the police. Seeing this, Ellemarra suggested that he collect the firewood. Bell agreed and sent him unchained into the bush with a horse-drawn wagon. That night, the increasingly nervous gaoler saw the lone horse wandering back into Derby, unshackled from its cart.

Derby residents were angry at Bell's stupidity but were consoled two weeks later when a traveller reported that Richardson's unit once again had captured Ellemarra before he had reached the limestone range. Relieved settlers looked forward to Ellemarra's return in chains. Days later, Richardson and Captain arrived with a line of eight prisoners, but Ellemarra was not among them. An incredulous Richardson handed Drewry a broken padlock explaining that Ellemarra, with apparently superhuman strength, had torn it apart and escaped.

It is almost impossible to believe that Ellemarra could have broken the padlock with his bare hands, despite his renowned strength, but that is how the Derby Police occurrence book records it. A more plausible explanation is that Jandamarra assisted in Ellemarra's escape. Jandamarra had known Ellemarra since he was a small child. They belonged to the same Bunuba country, which embraced the lands south of Bandilngan, and were no doubt close relatives. Jandamarra's family obligations would have outweighed all other considerations. It was in Richardson's self interest to conceal any rebelliousness on Jandamarra's part. The settler community was highly suspicious of Bunuba men working with the police against their own people. Richardson had done much to convince his commander and local settlers of Jandamarra's complete loyalty. He needed to. Without Jandamarra, Richardson would have been just another ineffective police trooper in Bunuba country. With him, Richardson was able to capture big numbers and reap financial gain through the prisoner ration allowance, more than doubling his wage.

Could it have been in that September of 1894 that Ellemarra and Jandamarra planned a military resistance on a scale the police and settlers could not imagine? The settlers in Derby and surrounding stations were tense. Ellemarra's escape coincided with plans to push five hundred of Emanuel and Forrest's cattle along the Bunuba limestone fortress to Plum Plain. From there they would be fattened during the Wet and sold to Blythe, who intended moving them into the fertile heart of Bunuba country. Derby was alive with excited discussion about the stock-drive. Never before had cattle in these numbers been overlanded via the hostile Bunuba lands. The settlers would not be deterred by Ellemarra. The rapidly growing mining population far away to the south demanded beef, and Forrest and Emanuel were in danger of losing the market if they could not guarantee the supply. They desperately needed to get the cattle into the Bunuba ranges before the Wet, build up the herd in the following year and then commence the lucrative transport of fattened Kimberley cattle to the Kalgoorlie goldfields.

The plan, devised while Forrest electioneered in Derby, was left to be organised by Meda manager Felix Edgar. Two seasoned Kimberley stockmen, Frank Burke and Fred Edgar, and English new chum Billy Gibbs, were hired to drive the cattle. Gibbs had just been rejected as a police recruit and relished the chance of colonial adventure. The West Kimberley settlers were buoyed by a sense of conquest, but Felix Edgar wanted no risks and demanded an armed police escort. Instead, Drewry, capitalising on the opportunity, planned a two-pronged police attack on the Bunuba, prior to the cattle arriving at the Balili range.

Guided by Jandamarra, Richardson would scour the Balili, aiming to capture Ellemarra and other Bunuba warriors, while Pilmer's unit would converge on Ganimbiri from the Fitzroy. The plan went wrong immediately because Pilmer's unit was in disarray on the lower Fitzroy. Two of his troopers deserted and he became hopelessly lost trying to recapture them. When Richardson and Captain returned to Lillimooloora in late September to begin their mission, Jandamarra was nowhere to be seen. After several days Richardson could wait no longer and commenced patrolling without him. When he returned empty-handed, he found a brash Jandamarra waiting casually. If ever Richardson needed reminding of his complete dependence on Jandamarra, he was made aware of it now.

The unit returned to the bush immediately, but this time with Jandamarra leading it stealthily toward an encampment on the

Richenda River. There, in a surprise dawn raid, Tillinberra, Teebuck, Muckenmarra and Tulbarra were captured and chained. The patrol then headed forty miles south to where Jandamarra knew a large group of his countrymen was gathered. In one devastating attack, nine Bunuba men were seized. Richardson also chained four women witnesses for the Derby court. The chaining up of women was common practice. They were never charged but were used to give testimony in court proceedings to prove the guilt of their menfolk. Their numbers also swelled troopers' claims to prisoner ration allowances.

Next day, at Ninety-Two Mile Creek, where the Derby to Halls Creek telegraph line meets Ganimbiri, an unsuspecting Lilamarra was captured. With the longest-ever chain-gang of Bunuba prisoners, Richardson was unnerved by the suspected presence of Ellemarra looming somewhere in the bush. He returned to Lillimooloora to learn that Ellemarra was just a few miles away with two other Derby prison escapees, Wonginmarra and Bundajan. Their camp on the pindan plain offered the prospect of easy capture. Richardson's journal records that he chained the prisoners securely to a boab tree and, with Jandamarra and Captain, crept through the night and pounced on the unsuspecting Ellemarra and his sleeping comrades. Richardson's mission was the most successful police-strike ever against the Bunuba. One patrol had apparently broken the back of their resistance and Richardson savoured the moment. This failed gold prospector, who had worked for years in loneliness on a sheep station, overseeing its economic ruin, and who was socially crippled by a disastrous marriage, now looked forward to public acclaim and promotion within the police force.

As if intoxicated by greed, Richardson kept all seventeen prisoners chained at Lillimooloora for the next seven days. As each day passed he calculated the financial reward he would receive in prisoner ration allowances. The corrupt practice of holding prisoners longer than necessary to reap the per capita allowance was tolerated by Drewry as a means of recruiting and retaining bush troopers, so long as it was done discreetly. Richardson justified his delay at Lillimooloora when he recorded in his journal that one prisoner, Wingerarry, was too ill to travel. To conceal the institutionalised rort, Drewry reported to his Commissioner that Richardson was the one too sick to travel.

As he waited, Richardson was blind to the intense pressure Jandamarra was under from the prisoners. Most were his blood relatives or men he had known all his life. Under the late October sun, the scorching metal chains burnt their necks and shoulders. There was no relief. As the days wore on, their bitterness toward Jandamarra increased. They goaded him about his Bunuba obligations and demanded he release them.

Amidst the noisy rancour of Bunuba men and women, Ellemarra's spellbinding influence came to bear on Jandamarra. Possessing the authority to pardon him for past sins, Ellemarra beckoned the young man home to his people and the law. This man of wisdom had seen the suffering of others who had lost their land and must surely have reminded Jandamarra of the cattle herd that now plodded relentlessly toward Bunuba country. The Bunuba were at the edge of the abyss. Only Jandamarra could save them.

The pressure on Jandamarra was almost irresistible, but it was Lilamarra's intervention that finally broke him. This former police trooper, who had attempted to release prisoners at Mt Abbot only two months before, called Jandamarra 'Wadu', meaning brother-in-law. No relationship in Aboriginal society carries obligations of sharing and mutual assistance more than that between a man and the brother of the woman he marries. Lilamarra's young sister Mayannie had become Jandamarra's wife. She was also Richardson's occasional bed partner, and from that convenient union, Richardson had fathered Mayannie's child, a young girl whom Jandamarra had adopted as his own. Lilamarra played on Jandamarra's honour as an aggrieved husband, encouraging his resentment toward the arrogant policeman, who was oblivious to a conspiracy developing before his very eyes.

On the night of 31 October 1894, Jandamarra, deftly and in silence, released Lilamarra from the chain. The men armed with a rifle and revolver, entered the Lillimooloora homestead breezeway and stood over the sleeping Richardson. Jandamarra's single rifle shot killed the policeman instantly, and then Lilamarra emptied his revolver into the corpse.

Jandamarra may have suffered personal anguish in the days leading up to Richardson's killing, but once he had pulled the trigger he acted like a seasoned military commander. He liberated the remaining sixteen prisoners, collected all firearms, including two Winchester rifles, a Schneider rifle and two Webley revolvers. Keeping some to himself he distributed the others to the two Bunuba who could use them – Ellemarra and Lilamarra.

Not having used a gun since riding with Armitage, Ellemarra was clumsy and frightened by the ferocity of the weapon. Not so Jandamarra; he was so adept with firearms that his marksmanship was admired by both Aborigines and settlers. Captain, arming himself with the Schneider, had little choice but to cooperate with the rebels. He later testified that Jandamarra had forced him to join the group, but evidence shows him to have been an active participant as the uprising escalated. The freed prisoners were joined by their many relatives camped at Lillimooloora. Fifty-five men, women and children now walked as one the short distance to Bandilngan. Here they waited in ambush for the drovers, who would inevitably bring their cattle into the gorge for water. Knowing the police tactics of surprise ambush, Jandamarra prepared to deploy them against the settlers.

Astonishingly, men such as Muddenbudden, Luter, Byabarra and Merrimarra, chained only days before and for years uncompromisingly disdainful of the settlers, now accepted Jandamarra as their military leader. No doubt Ellemarra, the gifted Bunuba leader, sanctioned Jandamarra's battlefield command as the cattlemen approached. At the place where a Bunuba group had hurled rocks down on Forrester ten years earlier, now another group lay in ambush, this time armed with guns.

On 7 November, Burke and Gibbs led the cattle along the dry Lennard River sandbed toward the refreshing water at Bandilngan. They were alerted to immediate dangers by their two stockboys, Georgie and Nugget, who were stunned and nervous after hearing of the Lillimooloora mutiny. Burke, the old Kimberley hand and former Lillimooloora worker, knew Jandamarra well and could hardly believe the news. He rode on regardless, probably wondering what the misfit Richardson had done to provoke Jandamarra's betrayal. Impressing Gibbs with his knowledge of Aboriginal behaviour, Burke spoke persuasively about the Bunuba and how they would have fled deep into the Milawundi range, knowing the police would soon come to avenge Richardson's death. So convinced were they of their safety, the stockmen did not even bother collecting firearms from the wagon driven by Fred Edgar, some miles behind.

Under the scorching midday sun and obscured by clouds of red dust, the beasts lumbered toward the water. Suddenly, the glassy pool reflecting the towering white walls was transformed into a muddy, rippling trough as the animals jostled one another to quench their thirst. The sounds of white cockatoos occasionally breaking the silence gave way to the bellowing chorus of invading beasts.

The four stockmen went ahead to rest where the water remained undisturbed. Against a large boulder rising from the Windjana pool, Burke lay back smoking his pipe, oblivious to Georgie and Nugget arguing over the freshness of footprints in nearby sand. Without warning, Jandamarra appeared on top of the rock, his Winchester at the ready. 'You wouldn't shoot me, Pigeon!' cried Burke, pleading for his life.[11] Old associations were now irrelevant and Jandamarra opened fire, wounding the stockman, who collapsed into the water.

Gibbs mounted his mare and hastily rode from the gorge amidst the chaos of stampeding cattle. Standing on the rock, the cool marksman fired, striking the fleeing target in the shoulder. As the horse struggled up the steep river bank, it stumbled; its wounded rider fell and became hopelessly entangled in the barbed wire of an old sheep paddock. There Gibbs died as Bunuba warriors charged him with spears. Georgie tried to rescue Burke by taking advantage of the confusion, but Muddenbudden intervened and speared the white stockman to death.

As Bunuba men chased the frenzied cattle into the plains country, Georgie and Nugget fled on horseback to the bullock wagon. Fred Edgar, who had not heard the gunshots from the gorge, was alarmed on learning of the ambush. He ordered Nugget to defend the dray while he set off to ride back to Lukin's station with Georgie.

Jandamarra pursued the two black stockboys on Gibbs' horse. He found the terrified Nugget, who meekly surrendered his gun. In a declaration of war, Jandamarra told Nugget that he intended 'only to kill whites', and demanded that he, Nugget, spread the word along the Lennard, calling for all station Aborigines to join him. He then rode on to prevent Edgar and Georgie from warning Lukin of the rebellion.

In a chase demonstrating his skills on a horse, Jandamarra caught sight of his prey near Lukin's homestead. Seized with fear, Edgar and Georgie rode at a gallop as bullets from Jandamarra's lever-actioned Winchester rifle whined passed them. Jandamarra stood in the stirrups of a horse at full speed and continued to fire, until the animal collapsed beneath him. Now Jandamarra knew that news of the rebellion would be relayed to the Derby police, who would soon come to retaliate.

He hurried back on foot to the Bunuba fortress to mobilise his countrymen in preparation for inevitable battle. As he approached the gorge at sunset, Jandamarra noticed billowing thick black smoke. It was the wagon, in flames and surrounded by a large Bunuba group, savouring the spoils of victory. The wagon had been thoroughly looted. The whisky was shared around with alacrity.

The next morning the men surveyed the rewards of their ambush. In addition to weapons gained from Richardson, the Bunuba had seized a sizeable armoury from the wagon. It comprised a Winchester rifle, another Schneider rifle, a double-barrelled shotgun and four revolvers. Also claimed were four thousand rounds of ammunition, four pounds of gunpowder and twenty pounds of shotgun ammunition.

With knowledge of the ways of the police and settlers, Jandamarra had set up a potentially devastating military operation. The problem was, there were more guns than people who could use them. With little time to transform the band of stock killers into a fighting force modelled on the police, Jandamarra embarked on intensive training, using boab trees for target practice. Experience had taught Jandamarra to expect a police patrol of five riding out from Derby. He planned to attack it, capturing still more weapons. An invincible Bunuba army would then destroy Lukin's homestead, achieving a great victory. But Jandamarra could not have anticipated the violent onslaught that his people would soon face. Settlers, long tormented by the image of the 'civilised' Aborigine returning to the wilds and leading an attack on them, had now seen that image become reality. Those who had pressed for a murderous military campaign against the Bunuba were handed a godsend. Let the government dare to stop them now!

EXTREME MEASURES

ON 9 NOVEMBER 1894, AN Aboriginal courier stumbled exhausted into Drewry's office in Derby and handed over a crumpled note. Scribbled by Lukin, it told of Richardson's death and implicated Jandamarra and Captain in the killing. Immediately, Drewry despatched Corporal Cadden and a black trooper to the Lillimooloora homestead. Since Drewry considered four or five constables and six black troopers adequate to deal with Jandamarra and his accomplices, he relayed instructions for Spong and Anderson at Robinson River and Pilmer's unit at the Fitzroy, to converge on Lillimooloora.

When Drewry went to bed that night he must have been excited about the militia he had set loose on the Bunuba. He may have thought of the aftermath of Collins' death a year before in the East Kimberley and reckoned that Richardson's killing would result in similar bloodshed. While he stayed in distant command in Derby, his troopers would wipe out the Aboriginal resistance, allowing Emanuel and Forrest's cattle to graze on the Bunuba lands.

Just past midnight, Drewry was jolted from his bed by frantic knocking on his door. It was Felix Edgar, who had ridden through the night from Meda Station to bring news of the cattlemen killed at Bandilngan gorge. The police commander knew at once that he was confronted by an uprising of significant proportions. Unable to get back to sleep, Drewry prayed that the Bunuba had not discovered the cache of firearms and ammunition on Fred Edgar's wagon.

Word of the rebellion spread like wildfire around Derby. Almost the total settler population of sixty gathered in the early hours at the Port Hotel. The meeting was chaired by long-term resident and store-keeper Henry Fields, who in the past had done much to give Derby a sense of community. He had organised social functions, captained a local cricket team and become the secretary of the horse-racing club. As the West Kimberley correspondent to a number of newspapers in Perth, he was the voice of Derby to the outside world. For a long time it had been a bellicose voice, raised against the district's Aboriginal people, particularly those inhabiting the limestone ranges and the Upper Fitzroy River country.

With an impassioned plea, Fields inflamed even further the already emotional crowd. The death of the three settlers was the govern-ment's fault, he argued, because the police had not been empowered to deal effectively with Aboriginal people. The meeting voted unani-mously to outlaw all the Bunuba living between Lennard River Station and Milawundi. Not one of them, the settlers insisted, should be protected by the law.

The resolution was telegraphed to the Premier, Sir John Forrest, who replied, 'Every endeavour is being made to bring the murderers to justice.'[1] Not satisfied, Fields angrily responded, 'The bringing to justice of three miserable blacks is not good enough . . . in avenging the deaths of Richardson, Burke and Gibbs. The whole district should be prosecuted.'[2] Alexander Forrest had already articulated the colo-nial view of the sanctity of Aboriginal life in his famous rhetorical parliamentary question, 'whether the life of one European is not

Main Street, Derby, c.1890.

Sir George Grey, the
instigator and leader of
the British Kimberley
exploration party,
December 1837.

Washing wool, Mt Anderson Station, 1915.

Mounted police, Derby, c.1898.

Prisoners labouring, Derby causeway, c.1890.

Facing the hold, waiting for deportation to Rottnest Island and Fremantle Prison.

Kimberley men waiting for deportation to Rottnest Island.

TOP TO BOTTOM: Coolie-style haulage, Derby causeway, 1897; Chain gang, Derby causeway, c.1890; Horse-drawn tram, Derby, c.1890.

Police party, Derby mounting yard, c.1890.

Station workers in the bed of Bandaral **ngarri**, Fitzroy Crossing, c.1890.

Baron John Forrest, WA Premier 1890–1901.

Joe Blythe with sons (clockwise) Arthur (Archie), Joseph William (Joe Jnr), Charles Christopher and Mervyn Frederick. Roland is absent.

Broome Police Station, 1918. Clockwise: black tracker Pilot, Mounted PC Melrose, PC Green, PC Flood/District Clerk, PC Trekardo, Sgt Spry, Inspector OE Drewry, Sgt Lang.

Pilmer's punitive expedition, Canning Stock Route, 1911.

Mail coach, Derby, 1919.

Barney, Jandamarra's brother, and PC Fletcher.

Sub-inspector Ord, Derby, 1898.

Typical natural shaft in the wall of Bandilngan.

Entrance to Bandilngan.

Bungu, the junction of Bandaral ngarri and Mayalnga, in the dry season. The sandbar at this junction has been a meeting place for Bunuba and Gooniyandi people to fish, hunt and socialise since time immemorial. In January 1895 it was the scene of a massacre by the killing party led by Police Inspector Lawrence.

Milawundi was a place for Bunuba people to seek refuge from the police patrols.

Sheep yard backing onto the wall of Bandilngan. This is a place of cultural significance where the conflict between Bunuba people and settlers commenced in the 1880s.

Ganimbiri from Galanganyja, wet season.

Lillimooloora Station (Limalurru) homestead as depicted in 1887. The living spring, Limalwa, is at the base of Balili behind the homestead.

Ruins of Lillimooloora Station (Limalurru) homestead.

Ruins of the Oscar Range (Ganimbiri) Station homestead.

Ruins of the Oscar Range (Ganimbiri) Station homestead.

Chaining rings at the old Derby prison.

The upper reaches of Bandilngan.

Ancient walls of coral
reef, Ganimbiri.

The western entrance to Baraa.

Top of Bandilngan.

Jandamarra's rock,
Bandilngan.

Jandamarra's cave, Bandilngan. It was from this cave that Jandamarra fired at the police force led by Sub-inspector Drewry — Jandamarra was severely wounded.

Paintings in Jandamarra's cave, Baraa.

Guinyja.

Two-Mile Spring,
Ganimbiri, near old Oscar
Range homestead, where
the police party, led by PC
Pilmer, attacked a Bunuba
group killing Jandamarra's
mother, Jinny.

The site of Jandamarra's last stand, near the western end of Baraa.

William Richardson's headstone, Pioneer Cemetery, Derby.

The graves of John Collins and Tom Jasper, old Oscar Range Station.

Moonlight on the Balili, June Oscar.

Danggu.

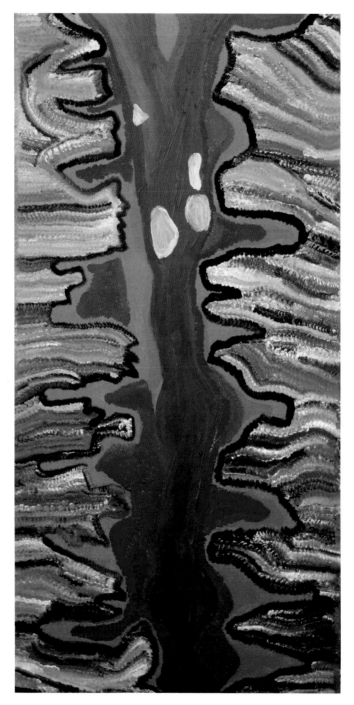

Aerial view of Bandilngan, June Oscar.

worth one thousand natives?' Now the West Kimberley settlers were openly demanding the genocide of the Bunuba.

Drewry's mixed emotions of panic, anger and frustration showed in his telegrams to Perth. Estimating the need for a party of at least twenty to confront the Bunuba, he bypassed Commissioner Phillips to pressure the Premier for permission to engage settlers as special constables, and to purchase horses. Trying hard to convince Forrest, Drewry reported Jandamarra and Captain to be 'the best shots over one hundred yards in the district'.[3] The comment was seized upon by the Perth press and incited alarm in the colony's capital.

Phillips was infuriated that his Derby subordinate should make direct contact with the Premier. In a dispute carried over fifteen hundred miles of telegraph wire, Phillips accused Drewry of acting under 'intense excitement instead of with the coolness so essential in cases of emergency'.[4]

'I am not excited and inflamed,' Drewry retorted, 'only annoyed at being detained here borrowing articles that should be kept in police store for emergencies.'[5] Bitter that requests over two years had gone unanswered, Drewry complained that his party would have to walk fifty miles to Balmangara Station before acquiring the horses they needed.

Knowing that Drewry's leadership was essential to quell the rebellion, Phillips was forced to encourage him, stating, 'I have full confidence in your ability to deal with the emergency.'[6] The Western Australian Government did indeed consider it an emergency. Premier Forrest met with the commissioner when first notified of the rebellion to discuss a strategy to deal with a situation that no Western Australian Government had faced before. Despite British Government scrutiny of Aboriginal-settler relations in Western Australia, legal constraints on West Kimberley colonists would be temporarily abandoned. The Bunuba rebels would be crushed decisively.

'Swear in as many specials as thought needed,' Drewry was told; the instruction ended a six-year ban on the use of special constables. Then came the long sought-after discretionary powers. 'Take such steps as you deem necessary to deal with the natives,' Phillips decreed.[7]

Despite Drewry's expanded authority, he was nervous. The uprising had happened at the onset of the Wet, when pastoral operations were scaling down and stations were short of white stockmen. Employing only one white worker, Lukin was most vulnerable to attack. To make matters worse, few bushmen were available as specials and Derby lacked men to fight the Bunuba in the ranges.

Sworn in as specials, Felix Edgar and drifter John Hamilton rode quickly from Derby along the Lennard preparing additional settlers and horses for Drewry's army. Their other task was to establish whether the Bunuba had discovered the guns in the wagon.

Drewry knew that military confrontation with the Bunuba would fail without armed Aboriginal support but he would not risk recruiting local black troopers. Just as Drewry hired horses from settlers, he also hired their Aboriginal servants, who had come overland from as far away as Queensland. Thomas Daly, a local teamster and stockowner, contracted out three of his black servants at thirty shillings a week. Five Queensland Aborigines had been hired before Drewry left Derby on 11 November 1894.

Derby settlers saw the uprising as a war declared. Following the Premier's directive that no expense be spared, the police purchased all firearms and ammunition available at Adcocks, the largest store in Derby. As this was still insufficient, the police encouraged settlers to hand over their surplus weapons and ammunition.

At Balmangara, half-way between Derby and Bandilngan, Drewry's brigade was reinforced by four white stockmen – Magee, Turner, Dean and Black. More importantly, Alf Barnett, station manager of Balmangara, provided six Aboriginal servants he had transported from Queensland some years before. That night, Cadden arrived from Lukin's station, confirming Drewry's worst fears; Jandamarra and his followers had seized all the firearms.

News of the rebellion caused great excitement in faraway Perth. In Parliament, Francis Connor demanded that 'retribution should be swift, sharp and decisive' and castigated the government for not supporting his Native Police Force motion a year before.[8] To calm the members, the Premier assured them that he had authorised the police and Resident Magistrate Warton to 'use every endeavour to bring the murderers to justice'.[9]

Leading the call for blood from the Perth press, the *West Australian* claimed: 'It is clear that policy, duty and humanity demand that a sharp lesson be read to the whole band of murderers.'[10] The *Daily News* blamed the government's previous inaction for the outbreak, claiming the killings had occurred where 'natives were known to be hostile, and yet little or no protection had been given to the squatters against their murderous instincts'. It warned, 'If any further settlers' lives were lost due to the arms the blacks now have, the responsibility must lie with the government.'[11]

The government's hopes rested on Drewry's leadership in putting down the uprising quickly. As the ex-mountie planned strategies for the looming battle, the situation could have been seen as a personal triumph. He had long advocated discretionary powers – now he possessed them. He was a persistent supporter of the proposal to introduce Queensland-style Native Police – now he commanded such a force. He was on the eve of leading a potentially devastating attack on an enemy who had fought for a decade. His chance for greatness had arrived.

But Drewry was far from relishing the moment. This was no ordinary 'punitive expedition', in which police would go out to kill and terrorise unarmed people with little risk to their own safety. Now an organised Aboriginal force, well-armed and under the command of a gifted military leader, awaited the police in their rocky fortress. This was a phenomenon totally unfamiliar to police and settlers.

Drewry's nerves were further stretched by Aboriginal excitement engendered by Jandamarra's 'call to arms'. The bush telegraph had spread the word quickly and, while some rallied to Bandilngan, most station Aboriginal people, who had seen too many of their family members slaughtered, stayed within the protective sanctuary of the pastoral homestead domain.

Drewry, becoming increasingly agitated, saw that British military chivalry had no place under the hot Kimberley sun. Hoping to kill Jandamarra and Ellemarra, he planned a pre-emptive strike. He knew that, without leadership, the Bunuba would be in disarray and easily crushed. Drewry despatched Barnett's Aboriginal servants to Bandilngan with orders to pretend to join Jandamarra's force. At an opportune time, they would kill both Jandamarra and Ellemarra. Failing this, their orders were to destroy the guns before fleeing to re-unite with the police at Lukin's homestead.

Documentary evidence provides conflicting accounts of the attempted assassination. Drewry's report has the Queenslanders telling their well-rehearsed story at Bandilngan on 14 November. All the time, a quietly listening but suspicious Jandamarra 'crossed them with his rifle'.[12] Ellemarra accused them of lying, telling them to leave or they would die. Yet, according to Drewry, despite the men's failure to kill Jandamarra and Ellemarra, the mission was productive. The Queenslanders were able to describe the Bunuba positions on their return and this, Drewry claimed, allowed him to plan an attack.

Charles Flinders, the West Kimberley mailman at the time, wrote in his unpublished memoirs that there was heated argument as Drewry and others planned the manoeuvre. Jimmy Black, Barnett's head stockman, argued that the Queenslanders could not be trusted and demanded to be allowed to accompany them. Drewry overruled him, insisting the mission would be jeopardised by the presence of any whites.

In his version of the incident, Flinders claimed the reluctant Queenslanders informed Jandamarra of the details of police strength and of their intended attack. Then they returned, swearing they could not locate the Bunuba leaders. According to Flinders, Jandamarra used this information to mastermind a well thought-out strategy. He broke up the Bunuba force into small armed parties and waited in ambush.

The weight of evidence from the unfolding of events makes Flinders' version more believable. Drewry was time and time again shown to be a liar. He wrote his journals and reports to reflect his position, even when it did not accord with the facts. He had a supreme ego and did not countenance dissent from people he considered subordinate. But he failed to command with authority because he lacked his men's respect.

Arriving at Lennard River Station on 15 November, Drewry and his heavily armed white and black warriors were confronted with the irascible William Lukin, who was furious at Drewry's handling of the operation. He was particularly contemptuous of the farcical attempt to kill Jandamarra and Ellemarra and refused to join the force, although he did supply arms to some of his loyal southern black workers, including the redoubtable Jim Crowe. The conflict between the two headstrong men erupted into a near brawl when Lukin refused to obey Drewry's directions to bury all firearms and ammunition.

Lukin blamed the rebellion on the police. He had always argued for two white troopers to be based at the Lennard. Five years earlier, in a letter to the *West Australian*, he had argued that there should always be two mounted constables on patrol to guard against an attack from defecting black troopers.

With a force of twenty-eight, seventeen of them black, Drewry planned to storm the Bunuba citadel in three separate squads. Under cover of darkness the parties manoeuvred into position for a surprise dawn attack. On 16 November, Drewry led his group twenty miles clear of the Lennard River and entered the eastern entrance of the gorge. In the still, black night, he and his men, without boots, crept through the gorge, taking position on the sandy bank where Burke had been shot only nine days before. It was 3.30 in the morning as Drewry waited for the others to take up their positions and enclose the Bunuba stronghold. In the murky dawn light, Drewry noticed Cadden's group creeping along the sand on the opposite side of the gorge. The two parties were placed well inside the canyon, increasing their chances of blocking escapes. It was the classic police operation, familiar to Jandamarra. He had either predicted it or been informed by the Queenslanders.

The early morning sun showed that the planned attack had gone hopelessly wrong. The police found nobody to attack. There was nothing but an eerie silence.

With brilliant military psychology, Jandamarra had enticed Drewry's force into a potentially devastating ambush. Hidden in caves and crevices were the barrels of twenty guns: repeating Winchester rifles, shotguns and revolvers, all aimed at the bewildered police. Nervous fingers on triggers waited for the command to fire.

From the narrow opening of a cave with a superb view of the gorge, Jandamarra directed operations. Just inside the entrance, before the cave broke into a web of tunnels, a huge rock sloping downwards into the darkness gave the command post the appearance of invulnerability from police bullets. Other armed fighters, including Ellemarra, Lilamarra, Muddenbudden, Luter, Byabarra, Wonginmarra, Teebuck and Captain, strategically placed themselves in the dark holes of the limestone wall surrounding Jandamarra's cave.

Jandamarra had thought of everything – except the possibility of his adversaries coming down the Balili rock face from the plateau above. Drewry's third party was made up of Barnett and Lukin's Aboriginal workers. Led by Jim Crowe, who, ironically, may have been shown this country many years earlier by Jandamarra, the makeshift armed brigade had on the previous night positioned itself on the southern side of the limestone plateau, at a place looking down several hundred feet to the Lennard River waterhole, where cattle had drunk only days before. At daybreak, they began their descent to assist the police at the bottom of the gorge. Scurrying down the cliff-face, these black troopers noticed the Bunuba positions and ended Jandamarra's hopes for a surprise ambush.

Within seconds, the ghostly silence was shattered by gunfire. Cadden's party of eight was trapped behind rocks, from which he was unable either to retreat or advance. Drewry, Felix Edgar, Bryce and others sheltered behind the boulders at the water's edge and fired rapidly at Bunuba positions to cover the black troopers coming down the cliffs.

Despite losing the opportunity of a surprise ambush, the Bunuba retained the military advantage. Police parties led by Cadden and Jim Crowe were marooned to the left and right of the Bunuba emplace-ments and could not expose themselves to fire. Only Drewry and his men, directly facing Jandamarra's cave on the opposite side of the gorge, could return the Bunuba gunfire.

With no gunman on either side willing to show himself, the battle developed into a stalemate. The Bunuba had avenues of retreat through limestone passages but the police were hopelessly snared. As the hours passed, the hastily trained Bunuba marksmen rained volleys of bullets onto their enemy. The Bunuba no doubt hoped that their gunfire and the hunger and thirst of their adversaries would force the police into error. The battle of Bandilngan became a deadly waiting game.

At 2:00pm, in the hottest part of the day and after eight hours of shooting, the Bunuba made a crucial mistake that shifted the military advantage dramatically to the police. In a moment of complacency, Ellemarra, who had positioned himself in a small crevice, slung himself downward across the jagged limestone wall toward Jandamarra's cave. He may have wished to discuss strategy or replenish ammunition. He was almost at the cave's entrance when a deadly wire cartridge exploded into his back.

Felix Edgar had fired the shot. It was a cruel, bush-made missile of heavy shot bound tightly into a solid charge and cocooned in thin lead foil from the lining of a common tea-chest. Caked with soap and bound with cotton-like wire, the cartridge remained intact over a long distance. Ellemarra's back was mangled, with torn flesh and shattered bones, but he managed to reach Jandamarra's cave before collapsing.

The effect was immediate on combatants on both sides. Word that Ellemarra had been hit spread quickly among the besieged troopers, whose morale rose instantly. The Bunuba were stunned. The invincible man lay dying, blood pouring from the gaping wound. Ellemarra had recovered before from settler-inflicted wounds. His escapes from chains were legendary; he had seemed immortal. But this time, the sounds of women's grief wafting from the cave's darkness told their unmistakable story. Ellemarra was dead.

All firing ceased. In the eerie stillness, the black troopers understood the sounds of distress and prepared to storm the Bunuba bastion. As the police rallied to take advantage of the chaos, Jandamarra forestalled them. He showed himself in full view at the cave's opening. With his Winchester firing rapidly he forced the cautiously advancing police into frenzied retreat.

Now Drewry knew Jandamarra's position and ordered a concentration of fire into the small dark hole into which Jandamarra had disappeared. Incredibly, he emerged minutes later with his weapon reloaded.

His rifle fire was continuous. As the ammunition from one weapon was expended, another was reloaded and passed to him by women supporters. A bullet pierced his shoulder but he held his ground and continued firing. Then two more bullets tore into his body, one hitting him in the stomach and another in the upper chest. Desperately wounded, he retreated into the darkness of the cave but continued to shoot into the sunlight.

A Bunuba victory was now impossible. A mass retreat began as one hundred men, women and children rushed along the tunnels and passages to the Balili plateau. It was an extraordinary escape, accomplished under the cover of Jandamarra's blazing rifle. Blood oozing from wounds, he held his rifle with one hand while supporting his body against a rock with the other. A bloodstained hand-mark testified to this courage and dedication to his countrymen, who had escaped to safety.

One black trooper called out that Jandamarra was dying, and the police charged. They shot dead two women before the attack and the yelling subsided. A disappointed Drewry then discovered that the recently formed Bunuba army had disappeared. The only evidence of the battle was spent shells and a pool of blood at the cave's entrance.

The police set up camp near the cave, believing that Jandamarra's vanquished army would emerge and surrender meekly. After some time, a terrified assembly of six women and three children were enticed from the cave where Jandamarra had held fort. Immediately, the women were chained and kept there as bait, under the mistaken belief that their menfolk would attempt a rescue.

By nightfall, Drewry and his troopers realised the Bunuba fighters had escaped. Next morning, he divided his force and attempted to hunt them down. One party followed the Bunuba southward on top of the limestone precipice while the other skirted the base on horse-back, directing those above. Shooting skirmishes occurred over the next two days as police occasionally caught sight of fleeing Bunuba. But always they escaped, taking advantage of the rocky fortress they knew so well. Drewry himself claimed the only further Bunuba fatality when he shot a young woman, named Terridine, in the back.

On 19 November, Drewry's exhausted force re-grouped at Lillimooloora. They were joined that night by Pilmer with two black troopers from the Fitzroy, and troopers from the Robinson River outpost. The tempestuous Pilmer, furious at having missed the battle, blasted his colleagues for their handling of the rebellion. He was not the only one annoyed. Discontented with Drewry's leader-ship, all the stockmen engaged as special constables abandoned the force. Drewry's battalion was further depleted because most of the Aboriginal troopers on short-term loan were discharged.

Felix Edgar rode back to Derby and telegraphed Alexander Forrest with the latest news of the uprising, and the plight of his cattle, now strewn for miles over the dry pindan plain. He also carried a message scribbled by the panic-stricken Drewry to Commissioner Phillips. The absence of police casualties was more to do with luck than military management and Drewry knew it. He knew also that, although he had the largest fighting force in Western Australia since Stirling had led his murderous army against the Nyoongars at Pinjarra in 1834, he still could not claim victory.

In three days of fighting, the police had killed three Bunuba women, captured nine women and children and regained two guns. All the other fighters had escaped, many with captured firearms.

Drewry's message shocked the government in Perth. Demanding ten Winchester rifles, ten Schneider rifles and several thousand rounds of ammunition, he added, 'the attitude of natives all over the West Kimberley district urgently requires that we arm specials at any moment."[13] What Drewry wanted was a massive military campaign against the Bunuba and other Aboriginal people, using an army made up principally of settlers sworn in as troopers. Heightening the drama, he urged that the Queensland government immediately supply a contingent of its native police troopers.

On 22 November, influential members of John Forrest's government met with Phillips to discuss the emergency. Drewry's suggestion of using Queensland black troopers and enlisting settlers as specials to form a Kimberley army was rejected. The political repercussions of such action were too risky. Instead, they decided to send reinforcements under the leadership of an experienced police officer to quash the rebellion once and for all.

Police Inspector William Lawrence, stationed at Roebourne, was an ideal choice to lead what would become the bloodiest campaign in Western Australia's history. Lawrence, at forty-seven, had spent most of his working life as a policeman in the northern districts. Unlike Drewry, this Bunbury-born colonial, who had grown up with the Forrest boys, understood well the peculiarities of Western Australian politics. Within hours of the Perth meeting he received a telegram from Commissioner Phillips, which read like a declaration of war:

> The natives in the West Kimberley have broken into open hostility toward the whites, and the police there being too weak to cope with them . . . You are to proceed to Derby, taking two Constables, specials if necessary, and six good native trackers with such horses, arms and ammunition as you can command. Upon arrival you are to assume control of the whole force and direction of the operations against the natives. In doing so you must be guided by circumstances and your own judgement. You must understand that the object of your mission is to free the district in a decisive manner and act promptly in the matter.[14]

Nine days later, on board the steamship *Albany*, Lawrence arrived in Derby with his party, consisting of police trooper Murdoch, Special Constable Sam Quill, a former Meda Station stockman, and six black troopers. Three of the black troopers had been conscripted from Roebourne prison, the others borrowed from a nearby sheep station.

For almost two weeks, Lawrence could do little but wait in Derby for the arrival of the steamer *Saladin*, hired by the government to bring up a large cache of arms and ammunition. The ship docked on 14 December, bringing with it ten Winchester rifles, twelve Webley revolvers, two William shotguns and several thousand rounds of ammunition.

The scent of blood infected Joe Blythe, who seized the opportunity. Rushing to Derby, this man, imbued with hatred, rallied the Fitzroy settlers as he passed through their stations, to prepare them for the slaughter to follow. At Noonkanbah Station he exhumed Lindsay's body, which he had buried a year and a half earlier. He carried the remains in a sack on to Derby for a symbolic funeral that would foreshadow a bloody catharsis. His time for revenge had come.

Blythe arrived in Derby to hold a council of war with Lawrence four days before the *Saladin* docked, and convinced his old Bunbury friend that the rebellion inspired by Jandamarra had spread to his Gurangadja property. He sported an ugly gash on his cheek to reinforce his story. With passion, Blythe described how he, his son Charlie and police trooper McDermott, had been assaulted by Bunuba stonethrowers at Danggu. The fact that the Bunuba were simply retaliating, because Blythe had just led a dawn raid on their camp and massacred seven people, was not told.

Persuaded to concentrate on the Upper Fitzroy, Lawrence arranged Blythe's appointment as a special constable to assist. On 15 December the party of ten left Derby amidst fanfare fit for an army riding to battle. On the town's outskirts they met Drewry, despondent and battered, riding in alone from the Balili range.

Leaving Pilmer and Cadden each in charge of two parties of ten troopers, the head of the West Kimberley police had rushed to Derby on hearing of Lawrence's arrival. In an abrupt conversation, Drewry informed Lawrence that the rain had begun falling in the ranges, making it almost impossible to pursue the Bunuba into Milawundi. Lawrence dismissed the Englishman as pathetic and rode speedily to meet his enemy.

Drewry telegraphed the commissioner, complaining angrily about his demotion. Phillips' terse response explained that Lawrence had been sent because of the alarming situation Drewry had portrayed after the battle at Bandilngan. Sounding like a supreme military leader directing a war from afar, Phillips ordered Drewry to return to his troopers, claiming, 'Natives are to be driven out of the district and operations are not to be abandoned on account of the Wet season. If natives can get about . . . so can the police.'[15]

When he arrived at Gurangadja on Christmas Eve 1894, Lawrence noted in his diary that McDermott was waiting with his eight prisoners chained to a tree. It was to be the last time he referred to prisoners in a campaign that was to last two and a half months. From the Fitzroy telegraph station he wired Phillips, 'Extreme measures have to be taken. Dispersing them is useless as they would return and commence depredations.'[16]

With Charlie Blythe added to the battalion, Lawrence led his men to the well-known Bunuba stronghold at Danggu. He appeared almost disappointed to discover that Pilmer's party, arriving there two days earlier, had massacred seventeen Bunuba people. The survivors had fled to the safety of Milawundi.

With the Bunuba in full retreat, Lawrence focused his attention on the Mayalnga area, the home of the Gooniyandi people, the Bunuba's close neighbours. He consulted the McDonalds at Fossil Downs about Aboriginal encampments, after which his party camped not far from a large gathering of forty men, women and children on a sandy bed of the Mayalnga. Using standard police tactics, the troopers surrounded the unsuspecting group just before dawn.

With guns firing, Joe Blythe and five black troopers charged them on horseback. On awakening, some of the Gooniyandi brandished spears in a courageous but pitiful attempt to defend themselves, while others ran frantically to the river bank for cover. In a cruel manoeuvre, Lawrence had positioned many of his men behind the trees along the river's edge to shoot those escaping. The carnage was over in minutes and afterwards Lawrence counted eleven dead and a number wounded. To emphasise that only men were killed, Lawrence wrote that none of the women and children had attempted to flee the police charge. There remained fifteen of them, all huddled together in grief and shock, surrounded by the bodies of their menfolk. Lawrence ordered them to retreat to Milawundi and not to return or 'they too would be shot'.[17]

Next day, Lawrence's party followed the tracks of the surviving women and children through the foothills of Milawundi, and finally to another encampment. Here the troopers shot dead three men, including Long Franky, a renowned and feared Aboriginal leader who the police said had once threatened to burn down the Fitzroy telegraph station. Realising that pursuit of more Aboriginal people was impossible in the rugged terrain, Lawrence returned to Fitzroy Crossing and telegraphed his commissioner, seeking approval to continue his violent campaign. 'Continue to operate against the natives but endeavour to disperse them with as little bloodshed as possible,' Phillips replied, with nuanced language effectively giving encouragement to fabrication in the reporting of Aboriginal deaths.[18]

By mid-January 1895, the tropical downpours heightened Lawrence's sense of urgency. Charlie Blythe returned to Gurangadja but his father remained with the party for the return journey along the rapidly rising Bandaral ngarri. The force was split into two parties of five, with Blythe taking the south side of the river and Lawrence the north. Concentrating on Emanuel's large Mt Campbell lease, the force then moved to attack Aboriginal people throughout the Fitzroy Valley. The troopers struck at all Aboriginal groups not living near the homestead compounds of Noonkanbah, Quanbun, Upper and Lower Liveringa and Mt Anderson stations. This was the Wet and many Aboriginal people had left the stations for the lay-off.

These were mostly Nyikina and Mangala people who had nothing to do with the Jandamarra-led rebellion in the Balili range. They were unprepared for the savage onslaught by Lawrence and Blythe. Clearly the Fitzroy settlers were not about to lose the political opportunity to terrorise the Aboriginal people into what they hoped would be everlasting subjection.

As Blythe led his troopers on the south side of the Bandaral ngarri, perhaps he thought of his father's participation with Stirling's army in the massacre at Pinjarra, south of Perth, fifty years earlier. There, Stirling divided his force to cover both sides of the Murray River to maximise Aboriginal casualties. As with the bloodbath at Pinjarra, the recorded death toll from Lawrence's campaign in the Bandaral ngarri valley was understated.

In the two-and-a-half month military operation covering eleven hundred and sixty miles, Lawrence reported shooting dead twenty-eight Aboriginal people. But Lawrence's official reports are not the only surviving records of the event. The story of the 1895 Fitzroy massacres has been passed down from those people who survived, to be retold by Aboriginal people today in vivid detail. Their accounts tally closely with Lawrence's diary except for the body count. This is how one old man on Noonkanbah Station told the story in 1979:

They were shooting all along this river. We can show you any time, you know. Bones laying just like rubbish. Right along . . . One would go one side of the river, and another policeman would go the other side. If the boys jumped over from the other side of the river, they got shot here. Right along, the Fitzroy. If he came out along a big mob of people, he'd just shoot straight in. He shot more people than we got living here.[19]

Feeling satisfied, Lawrence returned to Roebourne on 30 March 1895 and reported to Commissioner Phillips, 'It would have been impossible for me to disperse the natives without using extreme measures, some of them being a determined lot and to simply order them away, they would come back and laugh at the idea of being told to clear out.'[20] The settlers throughout the district were also happy and praised the government for the decisive response. Commenting on Lawrence's offensive, Roebourne's newspaper, the *Northern Public Opinion*, stated blandly, 'The blacks now . . . rightly understand the Mosaic law of a life for a life.'[21]

Jandamarra's armed rebellion had been used by West Kimberley settlers to inflict bloodshed on hundreds of people throughout the district. But settlers and police would soon be dismayed. Jandamarra and the Bunuba had not been defeated and soon showed that they were more determined than ever to defend their homelands.

RESURRECTION

DEJECTED AND DEFEATED, DREWRY REMAINED haunted for months by the nearly devastating ambush at Bandilngan. Settlers' reports describing the sub-inspector's incompetent handling of the rebellion reached Perth. His only supporter was Warton, the district's young resident magistrate, who wired Premier Forrest claiming, 'Drewry has worked splendidly, but his services do not seem to be understood or appreciated by Headquarters.'[1]

Drewry fought hard to restore his tarnished reputation. Despite the police failure at Bandilngan, he argued that Jandamarra's so-called gang was in disarray. 'They run like dogs, the excrement dropping from them whenever my party surprises them,' he reported to Phillips with a sense of satisfaction. Emphasising the collapse of the Bunuba fighting force, he even wrote that they had commenced 'to eat each other'.[2]

Most importantly, Drewry reported that the Aboriginal military leader was 'undoubtedly dead', despite the absence of a body. Jandamarra's death became his *cause celebre*. Collecting every skerrick of evidence, Drewry set out to prove it. Where Jandamarra had stood and fought there was the large pool of blood on the ground which, as one newspaper said, 'told its own story'.[3] Captured Bunuba women grieved over the seriousness of Jandamarra's bullet wounds, allowing Drewry to proclaim that his survival was impossible. After the Bandilngan battle, police identified the tracks of every one of the principal Bunuba men and women involved in the rebellion, except those of Jandamarra. Drewry also described a fight between Bunuba warriors over possession of one of Jandamarra's girlfriends and smugly informed Phillips that this would not have occurred had he been alive.

Drewry's conclusive evidence came from Irrawarra, a young woman captured two weeks after the battle. Under interrogation from black trooper Peter, who understood some Bunuba, she described the rushed funeral service of a great Bunuba man, and how the body was placed in a cavity in the limestone cliff and covered with earth. She was unable to utter the dead man's name, a customary reverence for the deceased. The wishful-thinking Drewry assumed she referred to Jandamarra. But no doubt the funeral she described was Ellemarra's.

Jandamarra had not died. After the battle he hid in a Bandilngan cave, where he was nursed by his mother Jinny and Mayannie, the woman who previously had slept with Richardson. When strong enough, he and his small family made the twenty-mile journey southward to Baraa, knowing that there he could recover in safety. Half a mile long, the cave cuts completely through Ganimbiri, with both ends hidden from view. Collapsed boulders obscure its eastern entrance while its western opening is shaded by trees and pandanus palms.

Food was plentiful. Fruit and vegetables grew in abundance near the cave and fleshy rock pythons and flying foxes were found inside. The free-flowing water of Baraa, fed by tropical rains from the Milawundi, supplied Jandamarra's family group with crocodiles, fish and crustaceans called jarramba.

During his quiet convalescence, Jandamarra no doubt became aware of the carnage wrought by the police and settlers following the armed Bunuba rebellion. News of the blood-letting at Danggu, where, in separate attacks, McDermott and Pilmer reported killing twenty-four Bunuba and Gooniyandi people, must have surely reached him. He would have heard also of Drewry's party attacking a large Bunuba assembly at Milawundi, where nine were officially reported killed. Some old Bunuba people believe that Jandamarra felt a terrible burden of responsibility that his actions in November 1894 had provided the trigger for the massive police offensive against Aboriginal people throughout the West Kimberley.

Besides Lawrence's campaign, troopers Spong and Anderson went on a rampage at Oobagooma Station, shooting dead twenty Warrwa people. The total number of Aboriginal deaths by police bullets will never be known. Official police records record that eighty-four were shot dead during the period of 'discretionary powers' between November 1894 and March 1895. The Bunuba were a minority of that official total. Unquestionably, the figure was just a fraction of the number who died.

The police offensive in the aftermath of Jandamarra's inspired rebellion was the most sustained slaughter of Aboriginal people in Western Australia's history. The bloodbath at Pinjarra in 1834 was a single event. The so-called 'Flying Foam Massacre' near Roebourne in 1868, sanctioned by Resident Magistrate Sholl, who swore in settlers as special constables, concentrated gunfire against one Aboriginal group. Aboriginal victims in the wake of trooper Collins' death in 1893 were shot by police only after the government had banned the use of settlers sworn in as special police constables. Yet in that West Kimberley wet season of 1894–95, the government gave police and settlers a licence to wage open warfare on defenceless Aboriginal families over a wide area.

Extraordinary efforts were taken by the government to conceal the extent of the carnage. Press coverage was heavily censored. Newspapers throughout the colony, including three daily and two weekly broadsheets in Perth alone, narrated the conflict from carefully selected police telegrams. In this closed colonial society there was little dissent or public disquiet over the sustained police offensive.

There was one notable exception. The *Catholic Record* in early January 1895 accused the government of engaging in a 'miserable slaughter':

> *The telegrams recently received from the Kimberley detailing the operation of the police against the natives will remain for ever as an indelible blot on the present administration. We trust there is no person in Western Australia who has not been thrilled with shame and indignation at the mere reading of this tale of blood, and no one possessing the rights of citizenship who does so with his whole heart protesting against the commission of such horrors in the name of justice and good government.*[4]

Had the West Kimberley Aborigines been of 'a different colour, had they been of a different country, we of Western Australia would probably be inclined to regard them as heroes', the *Record* argued. Almost tempting a charge of sedition, the paper concluded that many of them 'had laid down their lives to repel what they must have considered an unjust invasion'.[5]

Another quiet objector was not part of the humanitarian lobby but a member of Western Australia's social and political elite. His name was Octavius Burt, the younger brother of Forrest's Attorney General, Septimus. As departmental head of the Colonial Secretary's Office, he was responsible for vetting all police communications to the press. Disturbed by police telegrams, especially Lawrence's, he expressed his private fears to Sir John Forrest, 'that a war of extermination, in effect, is being waged on these unfortunate blacks in the Kimberley'.[6]

Forrest was also concerned, not for the plight of the Aborigines, but that the police military operations would come under the notice of the British Government and jeopardise his campaign to get rid of the Aboriginal Protection Board. His concern was soon realised. When reports of the killings reached England, the Colonial Office sent junior officer George Marsden to make subtle inquiries under the auspices of the Aboriginal Protection Board.

Livid that the enquiry was independent of his government, Forrest demanded details of Marsden's investigation from Governor Robinson and the Aboriginal Protection Board. Both refused to cooperate. In Parliament the Premier bitterly attacked the British Government and the Board, claiming, 'There was nothing occurring in the country, whether relating to politics or anything else, which should be kept back from the Government.'[7]

In the end, Forrest need not have worried. Marsden's report was a whitewash. While concluding, 'It was impossible to tell how many natives were shot by the police,' he stated, 'no shooting is ever done unless the natives resist, and then only as much as absolutely needful.' His only criticism of the police was directed at Pilmer for using an illegal cat o' nine tails which 'carried away flesh and skin at every stroke'.[8]

In the meantime, recriminations and arguments about who was to blame for the rebellion persisted. Soon after the battle at Bandilngan, Lukin wrote to Sir John Forrest, blaming the rebellion on loose security at Derby prison. Reminding Forrest of an earlier personal promise that all so-called intractable prisoners would be detained at Rottnest Island, Lukin credited Ellemarra for orchestrating the rebellion. Had Ellemarra been imprisoned on Rottnest and not at Derby, 'the whole thing would not have happened', he argued.[9]

Resident Magistrate Warton, with responsibilities for the Derby prison, rejected the charge as ridiculous and blamed the police chief for allowing only one mounted constable with two black troopers to patrol country known to be hostile. Drewry in turn maintained that Richardson had refused an offer for an additional constable at Lillimooloora, although documents show that Drewry had never intended to reinforce the Lennard camp.

The Bunuba uprising brought changes to some colonial practices. In late 1895, Dr Frederick House replaced Warton as resident magistrate. With instructions to implement Lukin's idea, he culled forty-four prisoners from Derby prison and transported them to Rottnest. For the next few years Derby prisoners decreed as intractable by the Resident Magistrate were shipped to the southern island prison. This policy was not restricted to Derby. As a result of the Bunuba uprising, magistrates at Wyndham, Broome, Roebourne and Carnarvon followed the same practice.

Jandamarra's outbreak ensured that, from then on, black troopers were recruited from distant lands. All locally-born Aborigines serving with the West Kimberley police were returned to their stations or to Derby prison. Desperately short of black troopers, Drewry wrote to Lawrence in Roebourne pleading for Pilbara reinforcements. Lawrence agreed and sent a crack squad of four black troopers to Derby.

Of these, Micki, recruited from a pastoral station south of Roebourne, was the most notable. Years earlier, he had been a notorious Pilbara rebel, stealing sheep and enticing servants away from stations to join his gang. An admired bushman, he eluded police for years until captured finally and imprisoned at Roebourne. On release he lived as a pastoral worker, although his rebellious spirit was ever present.

Micki's pastoral boss Lockyer readily agreed to a police request for Micki to be transported to the Kimberley as a trooper. There, he was assigned to Police Constable Chisolm, initially patrolling the Dampier Peninsula, north of Broome. In contrast to Jandamarra, Micki was transformed from rebel leader to police trooper, the most outstanding trooper of his generation. Two years later he and Jandamarra would meet in bitter battle.

By early 1895, Drewry felt satisfied. Squads of local white bushmen had joined his police force and Lawrence had supplied him with capable Pilbara black troopers. The Lillimooloora garrison of six, comprising Constables Bryce and Price, and four black troopers, would check the Bunuba. He was confident that those who had fled to the sanctuary of Milawundi would not return to the limestone country.

Now Bunuba country was on the verge of annexation into white pastoral hands. To convince Perth authorities that the Bunuba had been obliterated from the long-contested lands, Drewry cited the story of Wingunda, a Bunuba escapee from Derby prison. Despite a determined chase by the warder Bell, Wingunda reached the Balili range and found no trace of family members and continued walking southward along Ganimbiri to Danggu, the end of Bunuba country. Unable to find any of his countrymen, this stricken young man surrendered to Pilmer, pleading to be sent back to prison and to Bunuba companionship.

Drewry had managed to convince practically everyone that the Bunuba had been forced from their limestone strongholds. In early March 1895, the mailman Flinders set out to Derby from Fitzroy Crossing via Ganimbiri, the short route not used since the insurrection four months earlier. As he rode north along the telegraph line with the Derby-bound mail, another travelled the same route southward, heading for Halls Creek: William Phillips, a stockman-come-prospector. A social isolate, Phillips was known as a Mad Hatter, a popular frontier term to describe people whose long periods of loneliness generated behaviour unacceptable even by northern settler standards. Rejected by their own community, these men would look to Aborigines for sexual gratification and social warmth.

On the night of 15 March, Phillips camped at the Ninety-Two Mile Creek, a place he knew was a popular gathering site for Bunuba people. While dragging a woman into his tent he was speared through the upper thigh by Bunuba men. Next morning, Flinders found the victim in agony and rode on to Lillimooloora for police assistance. Rescued and brought to Derby, Mad Hatter Phillips enjoyed notoriety for having survived a Bunuba attack.

The spearing made a mockery of Drewry's claims that the Bunuba had been cleared from the area. Sheepishly, the Derby police boss asked for a reinstatement of his discretionary powers. Commissioner Phillips dismissed the request with the rebuke that there had already been 'enough bloodshed'.[10]

By early March 1895, the Commissioner in Perth showed that he would no longer tolerate excessive police violence toward Aborigines. He censured his troopers for their violence in two separate clashes. In the first incident, which occurred a few days before the spearing of traveller Phillips, Pilmer reported shooting a Bunuba man named Gorio who had thrown a spear at him. The spear missed but then Pilmer shot him, justifying it as self-defence. The commissioner rebuked him, explaining there was no need to shoot once the spear had been thrown and had missed.

The second clash was more serious. Lennard River troopers Bryce, Price and three black troopers attacked a large Bunuba encampment east of the Balili plateau, killing four. The death toll would have been higher had not most of the hundred-strong group been out hunting at the time. During the raid, a Bunuba man named Changarra rushed at black trooper Drake, attempting to wrest the rifle from him. In the struggle the rifle was broken before Bryce shot Changarra dead. In an attempt to justify the killing, Bryce claimed that Changarra had been with Jandamarra in the Bunuba uprising five months earlier.

The attack was condemned by Commissioner Phillips, who slated Bryce for leading it. Bryce, a former Kimberley stockman, sworn in as a special before the battle at Bandilngan, had been officially retained as a police trooper by Drewry. Phillips warned Drewry:

> Bryce may be an excellent bushman and an excellent hand at running down natives but he is ignorant of the powers of police constables and the regulation concerning the use of arms. If he continues to use firearms unjustifiably he will get into trouble.[11]

Commissioner Phillips had never been to the Kimberley. His only connection with the remote district was through official despatches or telegraph wire. Like others in government authority in Perth, he had grown tired of northern settler demands for the government to sanction the slaughter of Aborigines. The government had relented in the West Kimberley, but only after Aboriginal people themselves had taken up firearms. Deeply rooted in the traditions of the British colonial civil service, Phillips was not a military commander. He saw his police officers performing the traditional roles of upholding law and order. Police action following the Bunuba rebellion was, in his view, an aberration best forgotten. Since the conclusion of Lawrence's campaign, Phillips reasoned that Aborigines had been brought under subjection and should be treated once again 'with fairness and justice'.[12]

Far from being defeated, the Bunuba had returned from the safety of Milawundi to re-occupy the Balili range and Ganimbiri country. Following the spearing of the Mad Hatter, a worried Lukin wired the commissioner, pleading for another major police assault in the limestone ranges. Frightened about the large number of Aboriginal people living near his homestead under the protective status of 'station natives', he believed many would attempt to steal firearms and join their relatives in the bush.

Emphasising the continuing Bunuba threat, Lukin asserted that Jandamarra was very much alive and had led the attack at Ninety-Two Mile Creek. Lukin had no reason to doubt the Aboriginal people at his station. They claimed that Jandamarra was alive. Had Phillips been deceived? No, said Drewry, attempting to convince his commissioner that Lukin and the Bunuba living on his station were wrong. The footprints identified outside the tent of the Mad Hatter, he argued, were those of Byabarra, Luter and Jandamarra's brother Barney. Later, he reported that the 'Pigeon Lukin's natives talk about' was not Jandamarra, but 'a bird, or otherwise Barney, the police tracker'.[13]

The rumours that Jandamarra was alive became more credible by the day, but with no official sighting Drewry maintained his conviction that the man was dead. Few believed the increasingly discredited West Kimberley police chief.

Pleading for the reinstatement of discretionary powers, and clearly disturbed, Drewry telegraphed Phillips in late April 1895: 'I don't want to take an alarmist view of the situation but affairs are still very serious.' He explained that police had murder warrants for forty-seven Aborigines connected with the killings of Panter (1886), Rumner (1890), Dub a Dub (1891), Henry and Allen (1892), and Richardson, Burke and Gibbs (1894). More than half, he said, were associated with the latter deaths. Drewry stressed that police should not act only against those individuals wanted for murder, but also against those 'harbouring the criminals'.[14] Seeing the situation as one of war, he believed that police should be empowered to act without constraint against whole communities living independently of pastoral settlements.

Exasperated with Drewry's failure to suppress the Aboriginal threat during the period of discretionary power, Phillips responded angrily, 'If you say there are forty-seven natives at large implicated in the murders . . . why are you not in hot pursuit of them? . . . They must be hunted down and shot.' Leaving little doubt as to what he thought of Drewry's assertion that Jandamarra was dead, he instructed him, 'Every round fired must be made to tell. Random firing at rocks and mouths of caves upon chance of hitting a native is as useless as it is ridiculous and wasteful.'[15]

In May 1895, the Lennard River police unit confirmed the rumour that had been drifting into Derby over the previous two months. Jandamarra was alive. Two days later, Drewry resigned from the Western Australian Police Force.

Without firing a shot, Jandamarra had claimed the scalp of one more policeman. Soon, this young man would learn that he was held in such awe and fear by the police and settlers that, alone, he could hold back the pastoral advance into his country. While he remained alive and roaming the country far and wide, no settler dared stock the land they called 'Pigeon country'.

The fully recovered Jandamarra would no longer engage police and settlers in open combat. To do so would only incite an horrific response, with enormous suffering for his people. Rather, his tactics were to confuse, ridicule and exhaust police patrols. His knowledge of the rugged country made him feel perfectly safe. To police troopers he became almost ghostlike. His tracks were often sighted but nowhere was he seen. At times, Bryce led his police unit following footprints only to see them disappear over rocky ground. It was as though the land itself had swallowed him. And in a sense it had, for Jandamarra knew every cave, secret tunnel and crevice that riddled the rocky ranges. Increasingly, the police became demoralised.

Intricate knowledge of the country was one advantage; familiarity with the tactics of his former masters was another. Police scored successes against Aborigines when they raided encampments at dawn. They usually located the camps the evening before, by seeing the smoke from a cluster of camp fires or noticing the intersecting foot-tracks leading to the larger gatherings. Hence, Jandamarra avoided camping with large groups and so minimised the possibility of capture.

As a natural recluse, he lived and travelled with a small band of loyal companions. Among these were his mother Jinny, wife Mayannie and brother Barney. Captain, the foreigner to Bunuba country, stuck to him constantly but his loyalty may have been motivated by concern for his own protection. The group was highly mobile and versatile and able to hunt and gather food with ease. Young women outnumbered the men and acted as sentinels to warn of approaching police patrols. These measures gave Jandamarra an almost invincible alarm system.

Frequent false leads by captured Bunuba under police interrogation threw the hunt for Jandamarra into chaos, and sometimes the Bunuba used the police obsession with Jandamarra to their advantage. On one occasion, in August 1895, Bryce's police patrol north of Bandilngan pursued the tracks of Lilamarra, Carolon and other participants in the rebellion. During the chase the police captured and chained an old Aboriginal man named Illaigee and interrogated him in the hope of getting information concerning the whereabouts of Lilamarra and the others. The old man said that Jandamarra, Captain and Barney had been in the area a few days earlier but had left for Bandaral ngarri to capture arms and ammunition. After releasing Illaigee, the police abandoned the chase and rode quickly to Derby to warn of possible attacks on travellers by Jandamarra on the Fitzroy to Halls Creek road.

No doubt the old man's story was a deception but it caused fren-zied activity throughout the district. The acting head of the police,

Sergeant Cadden, telegraphed the police at Halls Creek and Fitzroy Crossing, instructing them to warn travellers of a possible Jandamarra ambush. All settlers along Bandaral ngarri and Mayalnga were told to hide their arms and ammunition. The district braced itself for another attack.

In Perth, Commissioner Phillips, increasingly impatient with the police's failure to capture Jandamarra and suppress the Bunuba, was briefed extensively about the state of affairs by private citizen Drewry. Drewry described the difficult terrain and the resistance tactics of the Bunuba so thoroughly that Phillips began to appreciate that this was indeed a situation akin to war. So impressive was Drewry's defence of his former command that Phillips not only reinstated him but promoted him to inspector in another district.

Jandamarra's mere existence continued to be a threat and caused settlers to complain bitterly about the police's inability to protect them. Again, the irate William Lukin labelled the Lennard River police incompetent. Soon after Richardson's death, the police had withdrawn from Lillimooloora to establish a camp near Lukin's homestead. There, Lukin berated them persistently, calling them cowards, and eventually Cadden ordered them back to Lillimooloora. Increasing Bunuba activity prompted Cadden to transfer Buckland to the Balili area, giving the outpost a total of seven troopers, the strongest in the Kimberley.

For Lukin, the commitment of police strength was too little, too late. A force this size might have brought the Bunuba to heel a decade previously, but now they were too experienced to be defeated in their own country. In twelve years, Lukin had seen his dream of carving out a life as a pastoral aristocrat turn sour. He had fought and over-come the dreaded scab disease that had threatened to destroy his sheep. He had survived bushfires, drought, flood, falling wool-prices and menacing dingoes. No other settler, swept to the Kimberley on the tide of great expectations, could claim to be more resilient than William Lukin. Only the Bunuba would finally defeat him.

One wonders whether Lukin reflected on the irony of his association with Kimberley Aboriginal people. When he had established Lennard River Station, his most pressing problem had been recruiting servile black labour. One of his few early successes was a young boy, whom he named 'Pigeon'. Ten years on, one hundred Aboriginal people nervously huddled around his homestead, knowing that there they would be safe from police bullets. But in the rocky Bunuba homeland only a few miles away, armed and invincible, Jandamarra was poised to strike at any time. For Lukin, the situation was unbearable. In November 1895, he left the Kimberley forever. He migrated to America and died in the earthquake that destroyed San Francisco in 1906.

In the meantime, Commissioner Phillips encouraged his West Kimberley troopers to finally crush those Aborigines who stood in the way of pastoral expansion. Pilmer in particular rallied to the renewed call for open hostilities. In August 1895, he followed foot-tracks leading to an encampment at Margaret River Gorge in Milawundi. No police patrol had ever come this far into the ranges. The unsuspecting group was attacked and nine were shot dead. Pilmer claimed they had 'turned and fought stubbornly'.[16] Reporting the slaughter, he mentioned their possession of a bullock carcass showing the McDonald brand. Weeks later, Pilmer's body-count rose by eight when he attacked a Bunuba camp at Dimond Gorge in Milawundi. This time his explanation was that the victims were Bunuba who had escaped his attack at Danggu a year before.

Commissioner Phillips found Pilmer's reports of these attacks 'very satisfactory' and advised Cadden that he wished to 'receive similar reports from the Lennard police, whose minds should be disabused of the erroneous impression they have of the censure passed upon Bryce'. To ensure that he was not seen as advocating genocide, Phillips qualified his statement: 'They have only to avoid shooting innocent or inoffensive natives.'[17]

In late October 1895, the Lennard police claimed a rare victory when Jandamarra's sense of invulnerability led to complacency. Relaxing on the banks of the Windjana pool, he and members of his band were oblivious to the seven Lennard troopers silently converging upon them. With guns firing the police closed in from three directions but, like a darting bird, Jandamarra disappeared into a nearby cave. Astonishingly, he managed to evade the blazing rifle of black trooper Jimmy, who fired his Winchester from only twenty yards away. Momentarily frozen by the sheer speed of the raid, Captain, fearing imminent death, then ran toward the police with arms raised in surrender.

Both Jinny and Mayannie attempted to flee to the caves but were trapped by the police and chained. All three captives were taken to the Lillimooloora homestead in preparation for their forced march to Derby. From the top of the range Jandamarra yelled to the police, seeking assurances that his wife and mother were unharmed. He was particularly concerned for his mother, whom he believed may have been shot. Excited by the prospect of capturing Jandamarra by trickery, the police invited him through Captain's mediation to come down under the protection of an arranged truce to examine the captured women.

The police found they were dealing with a skilled negotiator. Jandamarra's condition for entering the bargain was the release of his mother. The police agreed, maintaining confidence in their plan on the basis that Mayannie, secured in chains, would act as an effective lure. But the plan floundered when Jandamarra failed to cooperate. Jinny's liberation brought howls of mocking laughter from Jandamarra, who was no doubt aware all along of the treacherous intentions of his wife's captors. From the safety of the Balili plateau, Jandamarra watched helplessly as Mayannie and Captain were led away in chains. He was never to see them again.

Captain was detained in Derby prison until his trial in Roebourne the following June. The West Kimberley settlers demanded that he be returned to them and hanged at Lillimooloora so that a forced assembly of Aborigines would be terrorised by the execution spectacle. The settlers were to be bitterly disappointed. Predictably, Captain was convicted of the murder of Richardson and sentenced to death, but the jury recommended mercy. Captain's impassioned defence was that he was a foreigner and had been forced to join the rebellion by Jandamarra and other Bunuba. The argument was given credence by the style of his surrender. He maintained that he did not attempt to escape but ran toward the police, whom he saw as his liberators. Ignorant of the area's landscape, the jurymen overlooked Captain's countless opportunities to surrender following the battle at Bandilngan.

The Western Australian Executive Council accepted the recommendation for mercy and commuted Captain's sentence to life imprisonment at Rottnest Island. There he died in April 1897 in a measles epidemic, along with twenty other prisoners. No charges were laid against Mayannie. She was simply held as the principal Crown witness in Captain's trial and then indentured as a house servant to a prominent Roebourne resident.

THE SPIRIT OF JANDAMARRA

FOLLOWING HIS NARROW ESCAPE AND the capture of Mayannie and Captain, Jandamarra became more daring than ever. Over the following months, he harassed and taunted settlers and police in a psychological war of attrition. Here was a unique brand of guerilla warfare without violence. This campaign instilled fear and confusion into the minds of settlers and police.

With a touch of theatre, Jandamarra soon dispelled any belief that he had gone to ground. While trooper Price slept inside the Lillimooloora police quarters, Jandamarra raided the store house. Next morning, black troopers identified his footprints, marked boldly in white flour deliberately scattered on the dust. The message spelt both defiance and challenge – a statement of contempt for those whom he no doubt saw as clumsy and destructive interlopers. This was his country, a land of Creation heroes and ancestors who had passed to him an awesome responsibility to guard and protect it. The police did not know the country nor did they understand it. What is more, they were almost totally dependent on their Aboriginal troopers.

All four Lillimooloora black troopers were from the Pilbara. They were lonely, isolated and insecure without the leadership of confident police masters. Without effective black troopers, the police were helpless. Jandamarra understood the tenuous connection between police and their black troopers and aimed much of his campaign at that fragile union.

The police felt unsafe, even in their own bases. Jandamarra could appear at Lillimooloora in the dead of night, within feet of a sleeping policeman. Their constant fear was that this renowned marksman could shoot them at any time. The black troopers were even more nervous than their police bosses at the demoralised Lillimooloora garrison because of their fear of traditional law in a country to which they did not belong.

Lillimooloora was an ineffective police outpost, partly because it contained too many troopers. Preparations for patrol were always a major operation noticed by Bunuba sentries, who relayed messages of the patrols' movements. Not since the mid-1880s had police operations in Bunuba country been so futile and Bunuba tactics so effective. When the police split the patrol as a ruse or to cover more territory, they failed to fool their quarry. On occasions, Jandamarra stalked the police patrols, making them aware of his haunting presence. The uneasy black troopers knew that, somewhere out there, Jandamarra was waiting.

His dominance was near complete although, occasionally, police hopes were raised when it was thought he had been snared. Even then, Jandamarra's cat-and-mouse game was an important part of his strategy to wear them down. One time, a Bryce-led patrol followed his tracks into the eastern entrance of his Baraa hideaway. The excited patrol divided, each with rifles primed to fire at Jandamarra when he emerged from either entrance. After some days, exhausted and disheartened, the police abandoned the failed death-trap and returned to Lillimooloora. There they discovered that the Bunuba, in their absence, had broken into the police outpost and taken a revolver.

Dismayed, the troopers learned that the footprints outside their quarters included those of Jandamarra. Much later, the police discovered that Baraa had more than two entrances.

The police felt ridiculed and powerless. They knew that Jandamarra had at least one Winchester rifle and now had two high-calibre hand guns. Unsure how many additional guns he had acquired from other Bunuba after the 1894 uprising, the police were nervous about Aboriginal rumours that he had hidden guns in different parts of the limestone ranges. Their biggest hope was that soon his ammunition would be completely expended.

It became an obsession for settlers and police to deprive Jandamarra of ammunition. Bullets and gunpowder were buried carefully at Limalurru police base and at the border pastoral settlements – Fossil Downs, Gurangadja, Ganimbiri and Lennard River. It was a futile strategy because the ingenious Jandamarra could manufacture his own cartridges, using the gunpowder captured from Edgar's wagon.

He could make the lethal wire cartridge, the same type of havoc-wreaking missile as had shattered Ellemarra's body at the battle at Bandilngan. He also made cast earthen bullets. Into a hole dug in hard pindan, Jandamarra poured molten lead, which he extracted when cooled. If bullets made this way were smaller than the gun's bore, he enlarged them by wrapping thin strips of paperbark and tying kangaroo sinew around them. The sheet-lead lining of tea-chests was used for casting bullets, one chest yielding a large number of either .44 or .32 inch calibre shells.

The police knew they were confronting a man of exceptional skill. His own community saw him as clever, but in a way not understood by the colonisers. In the eyes of the Bunuba he had transcended from mortal being to someone blessed with magical power. In Aboriginal Australia such persons of high degree are accorded one of a number of titles. English speakers refer to such a person as a 'clever man' or 'medicine man', while common Aboriginal terms are Kadaitcha and Mabarn. The Bunuba said Jandamarra was Jalnggangurru.

The ritualistic process of gaining the magic power is highly secret. Those not members of the Jalnggangurru profession know little about it. These men are often loners and supreme egoists, exclusive with knowledge and tricks. Indeed, it is their aloofness and guarded secrecy that inspire so much awe. Magic is often demonstrated through elaborate trickery which, if discovered, would significantly reduce a Mabarn's claim to being the holder of great power. Jandamarra was no charlatan. His display of magic was overwhelmingly convincing. Neither the Bunuba nor the black troopers sent to hunt him questioned his legitimacy as a Jalnggangurru.

Bunuba storytellers today eulogise Jandamarra's commanding magical power. According to legend, he could 'fly like a bird and disappear like a ghost'.[1] In the face of the police Jandamarra showed his power of magic. Extraordinary feats of bravado and defiance of the dreaded troopers were, in the eyes of Aboriginal people, actions beyond the capacity of a normal human being. Recovery from the serious wounds at Bandilngan was proof to the Bunuba that Jandamarra was not mortal.

The Bunuba legend, which dwells on Jandamarra's immortality, says that he was two separate beings. His body was a physical manifestation of a hidden spirit, living secretly in a small soak near his Baraa sanctuary. The spirit, his 'life', could be destroyed only by another person of similar magical power. While his spirit remained unthreatened at the soak, Jandamarra could roam with freedom, knowing that neither police bullets nor spears from Aboriginal enemies could harm him.

Is it too much to suppose that the police themselves began to believe the stories of the invincibility of the man they sought to destroy? At times they were bemused by captured Bunuba who, under police interrogation, responded that Jandamarra had transformed himself into a bird and simply flown away. Certainly, the black troopers shared the Bunuba perception of Jandamarra as the 'clever man'. This did more to nullify the police operations against him than anything else; the black troopers would lead their police masters away from where they knew him to be. They knew the futility of chasing him and were fearful of his powers.

The police were aware that Jandamarra frequently visited his countrymen at Lennard River Station. Receiving a tip-off in late 1895 that Jandamarra was camped with thirty family members close to Lennard River homestead, Price and two black troopers stormed the camp at dawn. Knowing Price to be a clumsy horseman, Jandamarra lured him away from the main Bunuba group. Despite a desperate chase, Price firing repeatedly from horseback, the weaving and fast-running Jandamarra outpaced him to the limestone range.

How dispiriting for the police, for even when he was in their rifle sights on the open pindan plain, they were unable to kill or capture him. Jandamarra obviously relished the displays of excitement by the police whenever his footprints were seen on the flat lands west of the limestone range. It gave him yet another opportunity to toy with them and demonstrate his mastery. One time, an enthusiastic patrol followed his tracks toward Mt North, a lonely red rock pinnacle some twenty miles west of the Balili range. Jandamarra's tracks, like those of a ghost, led nowhere. The police were convinced that he had again outwitted them by doubling back to the safety of his rocky domain. Galloping fast in the dusk, the troopers followed Jandamarra's weaving track between ant hills and trees as they sought frantically to intercept him. In the glow of the setting sun, within view of the limestone range, the leading trooper was wrenched from his horse by a length of fencing-wire strung between two trees.

The trooper recovered, but the police had been humiliated yet again in this prolonged campaign of subtle warfare. The police desperately wanted Jandamarra to stand and fight. But in Jandamarra's war, the lives of settlers and police had to be spared. He would not present the police with another opportunity to unleash carnage. Instead, this Jalnggangurru man derided the police with bravado and magic.

Sub-inspector Harry Ord, who finally replaced Drewry in late 1895, was intolerant of his police troopers' constant failure in the hills. Like Drewry, he had undergone a brief police apprenticeship on the Murchison before his Kimberley appointment. Having arrived in Western Australia from Singapore only two years earlier, this nephew of former Governor Sir Harry Ord came to Derby with the goal of destroying Jandamarra and the Bunuba. Arrogant and ruthless, Ord had an impressive reputation as an inspector in the British Colonial Police Force, hunting down sea pirates near Singapore. Where Drewry and others had failed, he would be the one to succeed.

Despite his ambition, Ord was prepared to wait until after the 1896 wet season before preparing a strategy for running Jandamarra to ground. When the rains started falling in January 1896, Ord scaled down a heavy police presence at Lillimooloora. Leaving Price and black trooper Davey at the Napier outpost, he transferred Bryce, Buckland, and black troopers Billy and Jimmy to Robinson River, to help put down the Aboriginal raiders who threatened Alexander Forrest's Oobagooma Station. Price was happy to be rid of Bryce, whom he detested, and had just begun to enjoy peace at Limalurru when stockmen Fred Edgar and Peter Skeen, and their usually loyal black servants, Nugget and Bobby, arrived in transit to the Bandaral ngarri.

During the night, Nugget and Bobby absconded. Nugget's apparent disloyalty unnerved Edgar, who had taken many months to recover from Jandamarra's desperate efforts to prevent his escaping the ambush at Bandilngan. After the uprising, Nugget had remained loyal to Edgar, despite Jandamarra's pressure to join the Bunuba resistance. Strangely now over a year later he defected. A few days later,

Edgar and the others at Limalurru looked up at the Napier plateau and saw Nugget standing defiantly alongside Jandamarra, Lilamarra, Muddenbudden and others.

With the police garrison weakened, Jandamarra had changed tactics. His dramatic appearance signalled the beginning of what was to become an extraordinary siege: a fight for the very possession of Lillimooloora. For the next few days, Jandamarra and his comrades taunted the Lillimooloora party. Powerless, the tormented group waited in the hope that the other Lennard River police troopers would return in response to its frantic message for help.

Then, on the night of 30 January 1896, while Price and the stockmen slept inside the fortified Lillimooloora stone building, Jandamarra raided the store, pillaging all the salted beef and cooked rations. The garrison was devastated by the loss of its food. Sensing that the post was about to be abandoned, the force on the heights hurled abuse and threatened to throw spears from the safety of the limestone plateau.

Yet Price, the former London 'Bobby', refused to surrender Lillimooloora. Anger overtook fear and, with uncharacteristic courage, he crept alone in the darkness behind the unsuspecting Bunuba holding fort on top of the ranges. In the dawn light, Price stumbled clumsily onto the Bunuba group, and in fright blazed away indiscriminately with his repeater rifle. He shot dead one old woman and wounded two young girls and then retreated, after being hit on the elbow by a heavy wooden club. Bruised and battered, with bare feet lacerated by the jagged limestone, Price scrambled down the rocks.

There he found one of his victims, a young wounded girl who had fallen down the face of the cliff. The terrified girl was captured by the desperate Lillimooloora party, who seized the chance to make her a hostage, a bargaining tool to regain their lost rations. Jandamarra and the girl's mother soon negotiated her release in exchange for the food taken from the store the previous day.

Next day, Bryce, Buckland, Watts and four black troopers arrived to relieve the besieged Lillimooloora party. Edgar and Skeen took the opportunity to decamp immediately for the Bandaral ngarri. Bryce failed to understand how a well-armed and heavily fortified party could have been trapped by what he considered to be a mob of spear-throwers, and accused Price of incompetence. Furious, Price deserted his post and rode to Derby to resign, but Ord refused to accept his resignation, opting instead to retain him as a town-based constable. Describing him as a 'delicate fellow', Ord claimed he had 'plenty of pluck and would be a good man in a district where life was not so rough'.[2]

Following Price's departure, Bryce directed a series of police raids into the ranges. On two occasions, Jandamarra eluded capture by disappearing into crevices. Nugget and Jandamarra's brother Barney were not so lucky. Both were captured, chained and later taken to Derby prison. The Bunuba warriors adapted quickly to the police show of force. In the following weeks, Jandamarra and others continued to taunt and harass the police from elevated positions in the ranges in a concerted campaign to exhaust them.

Initial police anger turned to frustration and humiliation as the ritual continued from day to day. Jandamarra even benefited from friendly contact with some of the black troopers. Unbeknown to their bosses, black troopers on duty as night sentries supplied Jandamarra with information and tobacco at prearranged meeting places during the siege. The police discovered this and chained those black troopers they distrusted inside the Lillimooloora stone house at night. Yet the siege continued as exhausted police reached breaking point.

The abundant long grass flourishing in the wet season afforded cover to the Bunuba night-raiders, who closed in on the Lillimooloora homestead and bombarded the tin-roofed building with stones, giving the police little opportunity for much-needed sleep. During the day, police patrols were also subjected to stone-throwing by Bunuba, who had secreted themselves in the tunnel-riddled limestone ranges so well that eventually the police gave up following their tracks.

It was a creative siege – stones, verbal jousting and theatrical gesturing with spears was the style of Bunuba assault. All of this ended abruptly on 15 March 1896, when Jandamarra shot and wounded black trooper Harry, who had been ordered into the bush to hunt kangaroos. It was a sudden reminder to the police that, for all the innocent play-acting, Jandamarra remained in possession of the gun.

Commissioner Phillips was furious when reports reached him that the most wanted man in Western Australia was playing a cat-and-mouse game with a sizeable band of police troopers. 'Pigeon and party must be got rid of forthwith,' Phillips demanded in a stern telegram to Ord. 'The fact of his being at large is a disgrace to the police,' he claimed. 'Head the party and let us hear no more of Pigeon.'[3]

A chastened Sub-inspector Ord hastily led a posse that included Pilmer and black troopers Lumpy, Ned and Bobby. Pilmer, who just happened to be in Derby delivering a batch of prisoners from the Fitzroy, relished the opportunity to ride into battle. At Lillimooloora both he and Ord found exhausted police troopers in a most bizarre siege. This was a situation that did not call for conventional military confrontation, and Ord knew it.

Instructing all seven Lennard River troopers to patrol well away from Lillimooloora, Ord concealed his own party of five inside the stone building. The plan was that, when the Bunuba came down from the ranges to plunder the apparently deserted outpost, the troopers would surprise them at point blank range. To Jandamarra and the other Bunuba, who surely saw the plan for what it was, the troopers must have appeared ridiculous. For four days, the police party remained crammed inside the stone house, playing out the act of trickery without sighting or hearing any of the Bunuba. This frustrating and silent confinement caused Ord and Pilmer to resent each other for a long time to come. Spoiling for a fight with the Bunuba, Pilmer was not shy about expressing his opinions of Ord's tactics, which he considered cowardly.

When the others returned to the station, Ord, possibly embarrassed by his failed trick, commanded a patrol which searched an area of Bunuba country extending to the Leopold Range and Ganimbiri. Any foot-tracks were soon obliterated by persistent monsoonal rains and, after several days, the dejected party returned to Lillimooloora. As they skirted the foot of the ranges, the fatigued troopers were drawn to the sight of a solitary figure standing on top of the limestone plateau. It was Jandamarra. He yelled at them as though enjoying his notoriety, then disappeared silently into the ranges.

Returning to Derby, Ord reported his failed mission to the commissioner. He complained bitterly, saying the nature of the country and tropical rains favoured Jandamarra. But Ord paid his arch enemy begrudging respect:

> He could stand covered on the top of the Napier Range and talk to those men at hand at the face as if the whole British army were there and he would be absolutely safe . . . I have a first class establishment of men now, and if any of those could come across him they will account for him, but to do so requires strategy, time and chance.[4]

Jandamarra would not allow Ord the chance to prepare a strategy to defeat him. He knew when to withdraw from his high profile role of police-baiting. It was not just his safety but the security of other community members that mattered. The impact of a large police force at Lillimooloora early in 1896 undoubtedly evoked Bunuba memories of the gunfire of the big patrols after the uprising of late 1894. In anticipation of a similar onslaught, several Bunuba sought protection from police by adopting temporary pastoral worker status at Lennard River Station.

Kelly, Lukin's successor, counted over seventy Aborigines living at his station in March 1896, but only twenty-five were known to him. This Kimberley novice feared trouble and demanded police protection. When Ord told him that it was normal practice for pastoral managers to deal with these sorts of matters in their own way, Kelly pleaded that he was deeply religious and was unable to inflict violence on Aboriginal people. Ord then intervened and, under his command, a police party attacked the enlarged station camp, cracking stockwhips, shooting dogs and terrorising the recent arrivals, forcing them back into the ranges.

Jandamarra retreated into obscurity. For several months the police and settlers had no idea of his whereabouts. His footprints were not seen by patrols and the well-established police intelligence network provided no information about his doings. It was as though he had ceased to exist. This lull lessened the pressure on the police and on the Bunuba people.

In Jandamarra's absence there was a decline in police activity on the Bunuba frontier. The sense of threat to the settlers eased. Tom Jasper, a Kimberley stockman of ten years, decided to challenge the might of Jandamarra and went prospecting for gold in the Richenda River valley in July 1896. He was the first settler since the uprising to venture into the heart of Bunuba country without police protection. A few months later, he returned unscathed from behind the limestone rampart, as if to prove to his colonial compatriots that settlers could now travel the Bunuba country in safety. But Tom Jasper was renowned for his refusal to have regard for Aboriginal antagonism to whites and no other settlers at the time were encouraged to follow him.

Jandamarra's disappearance offered the West Kimberley police only a short-lived respite. Unexpectedly, the theatre of conflict shifted south to the Fitzroy River Valley, a region thought to be peaceful. If the settlers along the Bandaral ngarri believed that Lawrence's 'firing party' had crushed the remaining spirit of resistance by Aboriginal people, they were wrong. Tension between Aboriginal workers and the Noonkanbah Station management showed itself in May 1896, when a fight broke out between Noormadie, called Albert by the settlers, and a white boundary rider, Alex Duncan. Stabbed with a knife by Duncan, Noormadie was taken to Derby for medical treatment, and then imprisoned for six months. Here no doubt, Noormadie learned from Bunuba prisoners of Jandamarra's wondrous exploits in the limestone ranges.

Whether their stories inspired him will never be known, but in June 1896 Noormadie made a dramatic escape from Derby prison, taking with him five of his Nyikina countrymen. The escapees eluded the pursuing police and were able to make the long journey back to Noonkanbah. There they speared Duncan, who later recovered from his severe wounds in Derby hospital. Buoyed by a growing spirit of rebellion, both station workers and 'bush' Aborigines joined forces with the prison escapees to embark on a full-scale attack on white settlement along the Bandaral ngarri. Noonkanbah manager, William Cox, sought refuge behind makeshift barricades at the homestead with other armed settlers and enlisted black workers.

With the settlers confined to their homestead, the rebels lit a series of fires along a wide stretch of country. Quickly, the hot July easterly winds fanned a huge fire that raged on a fifty-mile front. The blaze engulfed the dry grassland plains of the Fitzroy River Valley as it raced toward the coast. The fertile pastures of Quanbun, Upper Liveringa, Lower Liveringa and Mt Anderson stations lay charred in its aftermath. Hundreds of miles of fencing were destroyed, but, amazingly, station managers reported few sheep burnt. In the confusion, black station workers fled, taking with them many station sheep.

For many days the winds persisted, propelling the fire to the mouth of the Bandaral ngarri at Yeeda Station and turning it north to threaten Derby. A billowing wall of black smoke raced toward the terrified residents. The fire extinguished itself on the edge of the mudflats, which almost surrounded the town, forming a natural firebreak. The much-cursed, mosquito-infested mudflats, the bane of Derby's existence, had saved the town.

Ord responded decisively to the insurrection. His hastily formed posse included Gus Rose, manager of Quanbun, the major casualty of the great fire. Over the smouldering, blackened country, Ord's patrol traced the tracks of Noormadie and his followers to the St George Range, south of the Noonkanbah homestead.

In similar fashion to the Balili and Ganimbiri range, these sandstone mountains provided a sanctuary to Aboriginal people. But the St George Range was like an island rising from an immense sea of sand and spinifex, and lacked the strategic advantage of the Bunuba stronghold. Ord's force, consisting of six black troopers, located Noormadie's group and attacked ruthlessly. Ord reported nine shot dead.

The killings were reported in the press, prompting calls for an impartial enquiry. Premier Forrest justified the police actions in parliament, claiming the Aborigines 'had formed themselves into a hostile camp . . . and threatened to burn the whites out'.[5] That seemed to satisfy the Aboriginal Protection Board and no official enquiry occurred. Noormadie escaped but was captured a year later and became one of the last Aboriginal persons to be imprisoned at Rottnest Island.

The police could respond effectively to the style of resistance led by Noormadie. Yet in the mountains of the Bunuba, lands still coveted by the cattlemen, a ghostlike figure kept the whites out. The police and settlers knew that Jandamarra had to be flushed out into the open where they could fight him. But how?

FIGHT TO THE END

IN LATE 1896, SETTLERS Gus Rose and Percy Hutton prepared to push cattle deep into the Bunuba homelands. Not since the 1894 uprising had such a move been considered by any settler. Now the economic forces made this invasion inevitable.

Leopold Downs, in the heart of Bunuba country, existed in name only. To stock it, Hutton and Rose planned to drive a thousand cattle, recently purchased from Emanuel, Forrest and Company, up the Bandaral ngarri, past Gurangadja, to the foothills of the Milawundi. Both Hutton and Rose were victims of the great Fitzroy fire and were now anxious to be cattlemen. Jandamarra or no Jandamarra, the herds would be driven in at the end of the 1896–97 wet season.

Using Jandamarra's existence as an excuse for open police hostilities, Pilmer struck ruthlessly at Bunuba groups in Milawundi. The carnage cleared the way for the occupation of Leopold Downs by the cattlemen. Joe Blythe, who still stuck to his vision of a family pastoral empire, saw the time as right for a push into the rangelands. In July 1896, after Kelly had deserted Lennard River Station, Blythe had installed himself as manager, gaining a strategic vantage point to prepare for his family's occupation of the contested country.

Prompted by Hutton and Rose, the shrewd old settler moved fast and began searching for a route over the Milawundi. His activities drew Jandamarra from his prolonged period of retreat. Stalking Blythe's survey expeditions, Jandamarra soon scared away the Aboriginal guides. The loss of guides normally rendered the whites inoperative, but the old bushman would not be deterred. He continued riding out alone, mapping the country, with eyes fixed on Milawundi, and dreaming of what lay beyond.

Blythe knew that pastoral occupation of the Bunuba lands would proceed only over Jandamarra's dead body. While he remained alive, the stockmen needed to drive the cattle would not enter his country. The siege at Lillimooloora earlier in the year had demonstrated Jandamarra's power. If he could keep a large police contingent at bay by tormenting them over a long period, what hope was there for settlers traversing the country in the open? The memories of the deaths of Richardson, Burke and Gibbs, and the knowledge that Jandamarra was still armed, remained a potent deterrent. Only those hardened bushmen of the calibre of Joe Blythe and Tom Jasper had the courage and determination to confront Jandamarra in his own country.

Blythe family tradition tells about the old man setting up camp regularly, with a small fire burning, then moving away into the dark of the night, either to sleep or to attempt to ensnare Jandamarra. The legend says that often Blythe and Jandamarra exchanged roles in a deadly game of hunter and hunted. While there is no written record that the two met face-to-face during Blythe's lonely expeditions, Bunuba oral history tells how Jandamarra once lured Blythe into Bandilngan and ambushed him.

After waiting inside a cave several hundred feet up the limestone wall at the entrance of the gorge, Jandamarra suddenly emerged, aiming his rifle at Blythe, who sat frozen in his saddle. The pathetic old man pleaded for his life as his long-time adversary toyed with him. Banjo Woorunmurra says that Jandamarra fired, deliberately hitting Blythe in the hand. A police occurrence book entry records Blythe riding into Derby on 15 December 1896 to seek medical attention for a bullet wound, with the explanation that he had shot himself accidentally. It may well have been that Blythe masked the real reason for the wound to conceal his hurt pride and to avoid enhancing Jandamarra's already fearful reputation.

Resignations of Bryce and Watts led to the changing of the guard at Lillimooloora in late 1896. New trooper Chisolm threatened the Bunuba little, but the presence of black trooper Micki shifted the balance decisively toward the police. Micki had been patrolling the Dampier Peninsula north of Broome for well over a year, earning himself an awesome reputation as a hunter. Chisolm, his boss, was no great bushman, and only a few years before had been tramping London pavements as a Bobby.

Perhaps, at the time, the police failed to appreciate that Micki provided their only real chance of destroying Jandamarra. Bunuba people today tell that Micki possessed the secret spiritual powers of Jalnggangurru. Unlike other black troopers, Micki was not afraid of the Bunuba legend. But more than this, his clever man status inspired him to match Jandamarra in a fight to the death.

Micki's impact on the Bunuba was immediate. Just before Christmas 1896, the police claimed their most significant victory since the uprising when Lilamarra, Jandamarra's brother-in-law and ardent lieutenant, was captured while visiting relatives at Lennard River Station. Striding across the pindan plains, the cavalier Lilamarra no doubt thought the police too incompetent to catch him. But he had not counted on Micki who, on hearing of Lilamarra's nocturnal visit to the station encampment, closed in rapidly, giving him no chance of escape.

The wet season of 1896–97 was not accompanied by the expected assertion of Bunuba confidence as in previous years. There was little stock-killing and the police and settlers did not sight the Bunuba in the limestone ranges. Referring to the Lennard River Station area, the regular Derby correspondent to *Northern Public Opinion* claimed, in February 1897, 'Natives are giving less trouble ... owing to a sharp lookout by outlying police.' It was a rare tribute to the police from the correspondent, who also maintained, 'A close run through their strongholds is often salutary for the natives. As in this case, the management of the stations has remained undisputed.'[1]

The police soon realised that their enemy had not simply disappeared. It seems the Bunuba had withdrawn from the Balili area, not from a new-born sense of fear of the police, but because dramatic events were occurring in the south-eastern corner of their country.

In early March 1897, a stockman named Hooper led a one-thousand-strong herd of cattle through the narrow Ganimbiri pass near the Gurangadja homestead. From there, he drove them some thirty miles north along the Bandaral ngarri where he established a camp, later to become the first Leopold Downs homestead. Hutton and Rose had finally succeeded. The heart of Bunuba country had been pierced.

The cattle invasion rang alarm bells throughout much of the Bunuba world. Country that cattle now grazed upon was enriched by sacred Law. It also cut the Bunuba world in two, separating those continuing to occupy the Balili and the Ganimbiri from those in the Milawundi. The balance of power in this long frontier struggle now took a sudden and dramatic turn. The settlers had broken through the limestone barrier and had established a cattle station behind Bunuba lines. No longer, it seemed, would the settlers be deterred by the creative strategy of non-violent resistance. The new circumstances evoked a hostile Bunuba response.

Nestled among clumps of spinifex grass not far from where Hooper had broken through the limestone ridge, stood the small but stately home of John Collins. This long-time West Kimberley settler had erected his stone house within half a mile of the silvery grey Ganimbiri wall. Built from local granite in 1896, the homestead resembled the fortress-style building of Lillimooloora. Collins was content with his small, fertile cattle-run, which he named Oscar Range Station. He had no expansionary designs on Bunuba country.

In his suffering from prolonged stress brought about from living on the border country, Collins looked forward to the formation of Leopold Downs, which promised to push the Bunuba north to set a new and safer frontier. Caught up in the excitement of the cattle push toward Milawundi in that March of 1897, he welcomed the disruptions to his lonely life. His homestead became a port of call to the odd stockman who ventured to the new cattle station, which the settlers dubbed Hooper's Camp.

Two of those itinerant stockmen were Fred Edgar and Jack Mayall. Edgar, who had an uncanny knack for being at places where the Bunuba were about to strike, was persuaded by a nervous Collins to remain to defend the house. On the previous two nights, Bunuba raiders had ransacked the vegetable garden and pillaged various items around the homestead. Never had Collins known the Bunuba to be so daring and he feared for his life. All three men were well-seasoned Kimberley settlers but they huddled together, anxiously awaiting an attack.

The tense settlers were relieved when Tom Jasper arrived with twenty Oobagooma horses en route to Hooper's camp. Deriding Collins and his visitors for hiding behind the homestead's stone walls, Jasper seemed unconcerned about reports that Jandamarra was close by. This man had already shown contempt for the settlers' obsession with their nemesis, by travelling extensively through his country without protection. Jasper was an individualist who believed that a white man should never show fear to Aboriginal people because any indication of weakness would invite Aboriginal assertiveness.

Consistent with his frontier philosophy, Jasper camped under the stars alone, despite warnings from Edgar, who remained haunted by memories of his escape on horseback from Jandamarra over two years before. Jasper camped that night close to the homestead, on the grassy banks of the gently flowing Two-Mile Creek, named for its distance from its source in Ganimbiri.

There, a deep rock-pool, surrounded by leafy pandanus palms, lay at the head of a winding gully through the limestone range. Since time immemorial, it had been a place for meetings and religious worship. That night, around the waterhole camped a large group of Bunuba men, women and children. Among them were many who had fought in the 1894 uprising: Byabarra, Luter, Bool, Muddenbudden and Jandamarra himself. The Bunuba fighting force had been significantly weakened by the loss of men such as Ellemarra, Lilamarra, Bundajan and Captain, but it had gained an outstanding recruit in Woorunmurra, known to the police as Dicky. At the time of the uprising, Woorunmurra was a police trooper, but he had deliberately kept well away from any conflict with his own people. He was later gaoled for absconding, but then escaped, was recaptured and gaoled again. On his release in late 1896, there was no question where his loyalties lay.

Jasper's act was not one of bravery but of arrogant stupidity, for which he would pay with his life. The still night was shattered by a single explosion. The gunshot jolted the three settlers into consciousness. Convincing each other that Jasper had perhaps shot a menacing dingo, they returned to restless sleep. At dawn, one of Collins' black servants banged at the homestead door, bringing news that Tom

Jasper had been shot dead as he lay sleeping under the cover of his makeshift calico tent.

Perth newspapers described in graphic detail how Woorunmurra had shot and killed Jasper, while Jandamarra and four comrades, with bestial lust, had mutilated his body with spears and clubs. It was the sort of anti-Aboriginal propaganda that came easily to Western Australia's nineteenth century press. The three settlers' testimony that only a gunshot was heard in the midst of an otherwise silent night invalidates the press reports. No autopsy was carried out and Jasper was buried near the homestead in a hastily arranged funeral service.

In misty rain, three weary men clustered around Jasper's grave. From the Bunuba in the ranges the occasional volley of gunfire sounded like a military salute above the eerie scene. From Jasper's tent the Bunuba had added to their armoury a revolver, a Winchester repeater and several rounds of ammunition. 'They have no shortage of bullets judging from the way they were using them,'[2] Collins would later write in the *Northern Public Opinion*. Newspaper reports created an image of a robust attack on the Ganimbiri homestead. 'We held the homestead and let the natives control the ranges,'[3] one article quoted Collins as saying.

There had been no attack on the Ganimbiri homestead. The killing of Jasper and distant gunfire in the ranges was not the beginning of another Bunuba uprising. There appears little doubt that Jasper's death and the theatrical gunfire that followed was meant as a deterrent, a clear signal to the settlers that a continuation of the cattle invasion would be met with violent resistance. Sadly, there seemed no basis for negotiations between the two peoples. One held grimly to the last vestiges of independent land, resorting to the language of symbolic gunfire in a vain hope that the other, a relentless invader, would somehow understand. But the settlers and police had long

shown that peace on this frontier would come only after the uncondi-
tional surrender of the traditional owners.

At the Fitzroy Crossing police station thirteen miles away, Pilmer
waited expectantly for news of a Bunuba attack. Recent Bunuba
movements in the ranges had prepared him for a rapid response.
Within hours of hearing of Jasper's death from an Aboriginal courier,
Pilmer and his deputy Nicholson, together with four black troopers,
were at Collins' homestead planning a devastating retaliatory strike.

Pilmer could hardly contain his excitement when he learned that
Jandamarra's footprints had been identified at Jasper's tent. Here was
his opportunity for greatness. The man who had missed the battle at
Bandilngan over two years earlier would now butcher the last of the
Bunuba resisters and claim the most wanted scalp in Western Australia.

Pilmer, possibly the most violent trooper in the history of Western
Australia's Police Force, was also a supreme egoist. It was clear he
fabricated his official reports to reflect his role as a military hero. He
even released his journals over telegraph to the Perth press. These
described his retaliation against the Bunuba after Jasper's death.

According to Pilmer, he and his police troopers waited all afternoon at the homestead as the noise from Bunuba gunfire echoed in
the distance. Applying tested tactics, Pilmer waited until nightfall
before leading his patrol into the ranges to surround their enemy.

> Guided by the scent of smoke, the party executed a skillful manoeuvre in
> an almost invulnerable natural stronghold, and succeeded in getting within
> twenty yards of 'Pigeon', who immediately opened fire with a Winchester
> repeater, delivering a shower of well directed shots which were acknow-
> ledged by such a storm of bullets from the constables that 'Pigeon', with his
> usual tactics, escaped through a subterranean passage, taking his rifle. So
> well was the attack directed that one of the principles (sic) in the Barrier
> murders was shot, while two others were wounded but escaped into the caves.

A survey of the scene after the fight showed that there were nine separate native camps with 'Pigeon's' camp, all cleverly located. Double-barrelled shot guns, a large quantity of revolvers, ammunition and an immense number of native weapons were secured by the police. In consequence of the dense smoke during the rapid firing, a native boy was wounded in the leg, and is now at the station, receiving the best treatment procurable.[4]

After further surveying the battle scene, Pilmer contended that the encounter was 'far more devastating to the natives than first thought.' Instead of one dead, he listed four, including Rowally and Murriman, both of whom were believed to have taken part in the 1894 uprising. He claimed also that Jandamarra was wounded and Byabarra had escaped with a broken arm.

There was no denying that a violent affray had taken place, but it was far from being a victory; the gung-ho Pilmer had bungled the police response. Jandamarra and other key Bunuba warriors dispersed easily, as no police reinforcements blocked their retreat. Ord blamed Pilmer for the delay in mobilising the district's police force, because Pilmer's telegraphed report of Jasper's death failed to mention Jandamarra's implication in the killing. Bitterly, Ord claimed, 'Pilmer it seems wants to be the hero that brings back Pigeon or kills him.'[5]

When Ord arrived finally at Ganimbiri Station, he examined the Two-Mile Creek massacre site and found bodies of women and children but none of the men whom Pilmer had cited. Among the dead was Jinny, Jandamarra's mother. Jandamarra had escaped unhurt and the tracks of others who were said to have been shot dead were identified. This prompted Ord to report sarcastically, 'Pilmer's natives have a way of coming to life again.'[6]

The radical Goldfields newspaper, the *T'Othersider*, ridiculed Perth press reports penned from Pilmer's telegrams. 'The narrator of the events of that fearful night of bloodshed was doubtless drunk with the wine of battle,' it claimed. So impressed was the *T'Othersider* with his military prowess that it suggested, 'Australian Governments mobilise Pilmer and send him home to Britain as an Australian contingent in case of a general flare-up over this Cretan business.'[7]

Far from being seen as a clever military performer, Pilmer was subjected to mockery soon after he arrived at Collins' homestead. Banjo Woorunmurra describes how Jandamarra acted as a decoy by withdrawing alone from the Bunuba encampment. He headed east, knowing that Pilmer would surely follow his footprints, clearly stamped in the damp black-soil flat lands. The tracks led to the Ganimbiri cliff-face at Guinyja. There the policeman, sitting on a horse covered in sweat, found himself hopelessly trapped and looking up at Jandamarra, poised with his Winchester rifle ready to fire.

The essence of the Bunuba story is that Jandamarra chose not to kill Pilmer. Instead, he toyed with him, yelling, 'Do you want your life?' Pilmer begged for mercy and the spectacle continued for some time until Jandamarra, with superb aim, blasted his hat from his head. The story paints Jandamarra as all the more heroic for humiliating rather than killing the odious Pilmer.

Meanwhile, in Derby, Ord soon learned of Jandamarra's actions and swung the whole of the West Kimberley Police Force into action. Conveniently, Buckland and Spong were in Derby delivering prisoners from their Lennard and Robinson River camps, making it easier for Ord to organise operations. So too was Joe Blythe, who demanded to join the hunt. While Ord, Spong and two black troopers rode directly to Ganimbiri Station along the telegraph line, Buckland and Blythe returned to Lennard River and black trooper Peter rode to alert Constable Anderson at Robinson River.

At the Lennard base an impatient Constable Buckland, with two black troopers, was ordered to wait for Anderson. Chisolm, black troopers Micki and Mingo, and Blythe with his loyal black servant,

Wisego, rode swiftly along the limestone rampart's western side. At Ninety-Two Mile Creek, just seven days after Jasper's death, they made a rendezvous with Ord's patrol. The following morning the combined force continued along the telegraph line. Approaching Collins' homestead, Ord found a note nailed to a gatepost. It was Pilmer's scribbled message, explaining that his patrol was pursuing 'Jasper's killers' north of Ganimbiri toward Baraa. Ord's fury at Pilmer remains indelibly scrawled on that letter: 'Still no mention of Pigeon!'[8]

Ord had intended to direct police operations with system and strategy from the military nerve-centre established at Ganimbiri Station homestead. Instead he found himself marooned there, not knowing the whereabouts of any of the three patrols supposedly under his command. Four days later, the angry Ord greeted Pilmer and his men, who arrived hungry and exhausted. Hoping to return to the fray after a short rest, Pilmer was humiliated by Ord, who despatched him and his troopers to guard Hooper's camp.

Pilmer and his men had been led a merry dance by Jandamarra and eight Bunuba women over many miles of rugged country. These women played a critical role in a strategy designed to outfox the police. They created a maze of foot-tracks, which continually slowed up the pursuing police. Acting as sentinels and food-gatherers, the women provided Jandamarra with almost invincible protection. Pilmer, 'newchum' Nicholson and four black troopers were simply no match for this fleet-footed Bunuba group.

The creative strategy perfected by Jandamarra in the country he knew so well had worked once more. Others implicated in Jasper's killing had gone to different parts of Ganimbiri, leaving a riddle of tracks to confuse the police. Jandamarra and other Bunuba had every reason to be confident that the police, exhausted and demoralised, would soon return to their bases.

Back at Collins' homestead, Ord despaired. Here was yet another humiliating defeat at the hands of a man who in his own country seemed invincible. Ord did not realise that on the police side was a man who possessed an ability equal to Jandamarra's. Micki had shown his brilliance when he ran down Lilamarra a few months earlier. Now this man from the faraway Pilbara district was on the verge of destroying, almost single-handedly, what remained of the Bunuba resistance.

On the morning of 23 March 1897, Micki led Chisolm's patrol along the perimeter of the Ganimbiri, intent on cutting Bunuba tracks. Watching from the safety of the limestone rampart, Woorunmurra, Muddenbudden, Byabarra, Luter and Bool perhaps wondered about the strange man who rode in front. Suddenly, Woorunmurra, the most talented of the group, showed himself openly on the pindan plain. Running fast along Mt Hardman Creek, Woorunmurra no doubt wanted to show that Jandamarra was not the only Bunuba who could confuse the police with cat-and-mouse strategies. This might have been so for other police units, but not one led by Micki.

Micki gave chase and within minutes the hapless Woorunmurra was run to ground. Leaving Woorunmurra chained in Chisolm's custody, Micki, Blythe, Mingo and Wisego turned toward the others, who appeared stunned at the speed of their countryman's capture. Within hours, all five had chains around their necks. Chisolm and Blythe could hardly believe their luck. The Bunuba resistance was in tatters.

Blythe, who had assumed control of Chisolm's unit, demanded that the prisoners lead them to Jandamarra. Chisolm's journal has the prisoners meekly obeying, but events indicate that their intention was to lead the police into an ambush and their liberation.

For three days, the police party of five, with their prisoners, searched the country north of the Ganimbiri, and finally sighted Jandamarra's footprints in the sandy bed of a creek, which today bears his English name. The 'Pigeon Creek' tracks led toward Jandamarra's Baraa sanctuary in the Balili and Ganimbiri range.

Jandamarra had, it seemed, manoeuvred the police into a perfect position from which to embark on a do-or-die battle. In the late afternoon of 27 March, the police sighted Jandamarra with his female comrades a short distance from the Balili cliff-face. The women remained unharmed as Jandamarra ran alone toward the limestone wall, with the police in pursuit. It appears his tactics were to draw the police toward the range and then turn to attack them with gunfire from elevated sniping positions. Firearms may have been waiting, secreted in strategic places among the rocks.

Jandamarra no doubt felt supremely confident about his ability to outpace the police patrol. He had done it in the past with ease, but this time he had not counted on Micki. Leaving his horse in the rocky terrain, Micki ran ahead of the other police, who were left well behind in the chase. The foot race escalated to a deadly shooting duel, with Jandamarra and Micki trading rifle fire as the Balili range cliffs loomed closer. Chisolm's journal records that Jandamarra was marked several times by rifle bullets, 'but without effect'.[9] Coming to dominate the contest, Micki fired rapidly at a fast retreating Jandamarra, who lunged desperately for the safety of the limestone range. Within yards of a thicket of long tropical grass that stretched to the Balili, Jandamarra fell under the fusillade of Micki's gunfire. He lay face down, still and silent, blood oozing from several wounds.

Micki stood from where he had fired, awaiting the recognition of his triumph as the sound of galloping horses drew closer. 'Well done Micki!' yelled Blythe excitedly, arriving first at the scene.[10] But he would not allow Micki the credit for Jandamarra's final destruction. Ordering him to stand back, old Blythe rode slowly toward Jandamarra's seemingly lifeless body. His would be the last shot to end this war, and then the Bunuba mountains were his.

Aiming his revolver at point blank range, Blythe paused, as if to savour the moment of conquest. Suddenly, the eyes of the two adversaries met as Jandamarra turned, clutching his Winchester. The noise of their guns, fired simultaneously, resounded against the limestone cliff. Blythe's gun hand inadvertently shielded him from a possibly fatal shot to the head. The bullet struck his pistol, shattering his thumb and one of his fingers. Jandamarra, hit in the groin, managed to propel himself into the long grass and disappear, leaving a trail of blood.

Near sundown, the police party could do nothing but camp near the range and carefully guard its prisoners. The excruciating pain of his second hand-wound in four months kept Blythe awake all night, sapping his fierce desire to see Jandamarra dead. At dawn, the police decided to ride to Derby to get Blythe's wound treated. At least they could boast five celebrated Bunuba prisoners and claim that Jandamarra, this time, had probably died. That, of course, was wishful thinking.

In the half light, Wisego nervously obeyed Blythe's stern order to harness the horses and prepare for departure. Minutes later, a single rifle shot shattered the still morning. Wisego was dead, shot by Jandamarra, who then stampeded the horses in all directions. Firing from different positions he forced the terrified troopers to seek cover behind logs and trees. This was from a man whom the troopers expected to be near death from the wounds of the previous night. For a time, the panic-stricken police had no idea where the next shot would come from. They were well armed, outnumbering the wounded Jandamarra four to one. And yet he had them cornered.

As Jandamarra's assault continued, the prisoners, tethered to a nearby tree, awaited their liberation. Ironically, the captives who had led the troopers to Jandamarra would now be used to flee from him. Forming the Bunuba into a circle, the besieged troopers from inside the human shield, searched nervously for their scattered horses.

Jandamarra failed to fire a single shot, obviously fearful of striking one of his own countrymen, whom he had sought so desperately to rescue. With horses secured, the police posse cut hastily through Barralama, just south of Baraa creek, and onto Galanganyja plain.

Slowed by the prisoners, the exhausted party pushed eastwards along Mt North Creek, before resting at midday on 29 March. Relief was clouded by guilt. One seriously wounded man had forced a heavily armed police troop into frantic retreat. Incredibly, it was not over yet. With the limestone wall in distant view, Blythe sensed the daunting presence of Jandamarra.

As blood flowed from his wounds, Jandamarra stalked the patrol over the grassy flat lands in a daring final bid to free his comrades. At any other time over the past two and a half years, a hint of Jandamarra on the flat lands would have seized the police with excitement that his capture was possible. But his psychological dominance was now complete and hastily the police mounted and continued their retreat. Jandamarra continued to follow as the troopers forced their captives into a fast walk. With relief they hurried toward the smoke of a lunch-time campfire that signalled the arrival of Police Constables Buckland and Anderson, and two black troopers.

The police ascendancy was restored. While Blythe continued to Derby with black trooper Mingo escorting the prisoners, the others followed Jandamarra's blood trail leading to the closest point in the Balili range. Again, Jandamarra became the hunted.

Arriving in Derby, Blythe telegraphed Ord at Fitzroy Crossing, describing the dramatic clash with Jandamarra in the Balili. Across telegraph wire, Blythe attempted to direct operations in a desperate bid to end Jandamarra's reign of resistance. Expecting Jandamarra to flee to the safe refuge of Gunbi (Mt Broome), Blythe pleaded with Ord to head north to intercept him. But Ord, with four troopers under his command, decided to await the arrival of reinforcements before striking out to confront this solitary and severely wounded enemy.

Blythe, better than any other white man, knew Jandamarra. He also knew the Bunuba country and Jandamarra's ability to use it for refuge against incredible odds. The police patrols that had scaled the limestone country in the wake of Jasper's killing had caused all the Bunuba to flee to the safety of the Leopold Ranges.

The limestone escarpment of the Balili and Ganimbiri ranges was now almost silent of Bunuba life. The only human sound was the rasping breath of the severely wounded Jandamarra, as he clawed his way southward along the Balili plateau, and the movement of the police patrols, which skirted the foot of both sides of the range.

From the Balili heights, Jandamarra had a clear view of the dark blue Milawundi ranges, less than thirty miles to the east. There he would be safe from the marauding police parties he could hear so clearly in the stillness of the night. It was now impossible for him to abandon the limestone rampart. Chisolm's patrol had cut through McSherry's Gap and was riding slowly down the eastern side. This patrol would intercept his tracks if he dared to make a break for the sanctuary of the ranges.

The women who had provided such essential support for so long had fled with other members of the surviving Bunuba. Jandamarra desperately needed their help. It was the women, his mother Jinny, Mayannie and others, who had nursed him back to health following his horrific wounding at Bandilngan gorge two and a half years earlier. But now his mother was dead and Mayannie imprisoned in a distant white world. If he were to strike out in the open and attempt to reach Milawundi he would need the women to slow the pursuing police. This tried and tested tactic would confuse the police as various foot-tracks led in different directions. His female companions would also collect food and bush medicine and keep a lookout.

Now, Jandamarra was completely alone. At another time he may have doubled back toward Bandilngan, evading the police who were moving in for the kill. This he had done many times, with an ease that barely challenged him. Exhausted and bleeding from several bullet wounds, Jandamarra confronted a man of equal power. While the police patrols skirted the foot of both sides of the Balili, Micki followed Jandamarra's blood trail, with the Baraa creek sanctuary looming closer and closer.

Jandamarra's will to fight on was fading rapidly. The odds were now overwhelming. His country was being invaded by cattlemen and few fighters remained to support the resistance. Most of his countrymen were dead or in chains. For three days he struggled along the Balili range plateau, resting in the myriad caves and crevices he knew so well. Despite exhaustion he still managed to outfox a police party of seven strong. Inch by inch he clawed his way toward his Baraa home.

Under the cover of darkness, with a trail of blood left along the Balili plateau, Jandamarra crawled into the safety of his cave sanctuary. There he might wait for months and recover, just as he had done over two years before. But this was not to be.

Outside waited his Aboriginal adversary, the man who the legend claims, knew the secrets of Jandamarra's immortality. As the sun rose on the morning of 1 April 1897, Jandamarra collected his Winchester and his few remaining bullets and walked into the daylight to meet him. He climbed to the top of a limestone pillar near the opening of his Baraa home. He stood there stoically, looking down at the statue-like figure of Micki, who waited patiently near a large boab tree.

For a moment, their eyes met in mutual respect, before the silence was broken by the blast of Jandamarra's rifle fire. His bullet pierced the boab, which Micki was using as a shield. Then, Micki took careful aim at his still target and fired. Jandamarra staggered and then plummeted over the side, more than one hundred feet to the ground.

The gunfire aroused the attention of the white troopers, who galloped to the scene. Turning over the body lying face down in the dust, Anderson and Buckland could hardly contain their excitement. Jandamarra was dead.

Micki's role in Jandamarra's death was suddenly cast aside. The white police would claim the credit and the accolades. Yet they knew that nobody would believe that Jandamarra was dead without evidence. They hacked off his head with a tomahawk in a symbolic act of victory, and rode to Lillimooloora. There they joined Ord's police party and celebrated their success. Before returning to Derby, Ord exhumed the corpse of Bill Richardson, which lay in a lonely unmarked grave, not far from where he was killed in October 1894.

Ord and his troopers returned to Derby to a hero's welcome. In a drunken night of celebration, their gruesome booty was displayed for all to see. Next morning, all of Derby's white residents, in a more sombre mood, gathered for the formal burial of Police Constable William Richardson: a delayed ceremony acknowledging the final revenge. Richardson's was the largest headstone ever to stand in the Derby cemetery. Close by was a more modest but enduring headstone of Lindsay Blythe.

In Perth, there was enormous interest in Jandamarra's head. Within weeks, so-called civilised people formed long queues and paid money to glimpse the skull of the notorious 'primitive' warrior. However, Perth people were tricked. The skull was not that of Jandamarra but of Wisego. Jandamarra's skull had been sent to England as a trophy for a famous arms manufacturer, William Ceener.

At Balili, Jandamarra's family returned from the Milawundi range to find Jandamarra's body. They placed the corpse in a boab tree, later wrapping it in paperbark and stowing it forever in a cave in the limestone cliff.

EPILOGUE

AUSTRALIAN HISTORY HAS LARGELY BEEN written by the conquerors. That dictum applies powerfully to the story of Jandamarra and the Bunuba resistance. The barbarism of the colonisers knew no bounds. Jandamarra and hundreds of his countrymen were slaughtered and their lands occupied. The survivors and their descendants worked for many decades as servants for the cattle barons. As if that were not enough, the Bunuba were to suffer a final injustice. Their own history was stolen and replaced by a lie.

This is how the Commissioner of Police reported the events surrounding the Jandamarra outbreak to the Western Australian Government in September 1897:

> For a lengthened period the settlers in the West Kimberley have been kept in a state of anxiety and alarm through the depredations and outrages of a tribe of lawless natives, inhabiting the Oscar and Barrier [Napier] Ranges, headed by a semi-civilised Aborigine called Pigeon, at one time employed by the police as native tracker.
>
> The trouble commenced in October 1894 with the murder of Constable Richardson, followed at a subsequent period by the murder of Messrs Burke

and Gibbs, and culminating on 15 March last in the murder of Thomas
Jasper at Collins' station, Oscar Range.

The inaccessible nature of the ranges rendered the task of following
the natives a difficult and arduous one, which almost invariably had to
be performed on foot. Moreover, in their various raids and murders, the
fugitives had secured a large quantity of arms and ammunition, which
they on every occasion preferred to use in resisting capture. Unsuccessful
efforts to recapture Pigeon and his gang were made by the police from
time to time until the murder of Thos. Jasper, when the members of
the force stationed at the Fitzroy, Lennard and Robinson camps with
the assistance of Mr Jos. Blythe turned out; and under the direction of
Sub-inspector Ord, completely rid the Oscar and Barrier Ranges of the
hostile tribe, capturing five of Mr Jasper's murderers and shooting Pigeon
dead on 1 April last. The natives arrested have since been tried at Derby
and convicted of murder.

I now beg to recommend that I be authorised to pay each of the five
constables named below, who were actually under fire, and who showed
great tact, perseverance, and courage in the pursuit of the offenders a
gratuity of £10.00 from the police reward fund, vis —

Constable Richard Pilmer
"   Hugh R Chisolm
"   AH Buckland
"   HR Anderson
"   Joseph Nicholson

I also propose with the sanction of the Honourable the Colonial Secretary
to award a gratuity of £5.00 to Constable AN Spong who performed useful
work under Sub-inspector Ord's instructions while the pursuit lasted
although he did not come directly in contact with the offenders.

The services rendered by Mr Jos. Blythe who accompanied the police
form the subject of another file. (Blythe would later be awarded £100.00 by
the government as compensation for the loss of his thumb.)

To each of the native trackers who assisted in the dispersal and capture
of the gang, I would suggest that goods to the value of £1 may be given,
consisting of such articles as will prove useful to them. The number of
trackers engaged was ten.

Commissioner of Police

22 Sept 1897

The police version of events is blatant propaganda, a perversion of history that came to be seen as fact. Firstly, it fails to acknowledge that the land violently contested belonged from time immemorial to the Bunuba. In stating that the problem commenced with the killing of Richardson in October 1894, it denies the many years of Bunuba resistance prior to the armed uprising.

While the police report dwells heavily on the deaths of one police trooper and three stockmen, it fails to mention the slaughter of hundreds of Aboriginal people during the 1894 and 1897. The carnage which Jandamarra's outbreak provoked was not restricted to the Bunuba but included the mass killings of countless men, women and children throughout the West Kimberley. People speaking the languages of Nyikina, Unggumi, Mangala, Gooniyandi and Warrwa suffered terribly when police and settlers were given unchecked powers to inflict mass destruction on a defenceless people.

The official version of the 1890s West Kimberley conflict, reproduced in popular mythology over the generations, was that Jandamarra and his Bunuba clansmen were outlaws, and the police and settlers responded to enforce the law. Nowhere was it described as military conflict, with the settlers intent on destroying the traditional owners of the land so that pastoral expansion could advance. Yet that was what it was. The escalation to armed resistance by the Bunuba in 1894 created the political circumstances for a holocaust against a people determined to protect their culture and traditions.

The suggestion that Jandamarra and the Bunuba were violent people possessing a lust to kill settlers and police was political misinformation designed to paint the victims as the aggressors. This interpretation of historical events does not stand up in the face of historical documents written by the colonisers themselves. What is surprising is that so few whites died, despite Jandamarra and others possessing arms. There is no doubt that Jandamarra deliberately chose not to take the lives of settlers and police, for which he had ample opportunity, after the killings of Richardson, Burke and Gibbs. Instead, he used creative, non-violent strategies.

Following the death of Jandamarra, pastoralists with their cattle moved quickly to occupy Bunuba lands and beyond. Leopold Station was established and Brooking Springs expanded to absorb Oscar Range Station in 1905, when John Collins died. Joe Blythe saw his dream of establishing a family cattle empire on Bunuba country come true. In addition to Brooking Springs, Mt House, Mt Hart, Glenroy and Mornington stations were established under the control and management of the Blythes. Early in the twentieth century, the Blythes also set up Fairfield Station, which took up most of the former Lillimooloora lease and the country that Jandamarra had defended to his death.

Throughout most of the twentieth century, Bunuba people lived and worked on those stations. They, like Aboriginal people on other stations in the Kimberley, were the backbone of the pastoral industry. Without them the pastoralists could never have made the money they did. The Bunuba saw pastoralists and their managers come and go. The Blythe descendants, after a failed economic experiment flying slaughtered cattle to market from a meatworks in their mountainous pastoral domains in the late 1940s and early '50s, sold their leases. Mt House was sold in the late '60s and so ended the Blythe presence in the Kimberley.

Following the equal wage award for pastoral workers in 1968, pastoralists, claiming they could no longer afford to maintain workers and their families, began pressuring the Bunuba to leave.

By the late 1970s, few Bunuba people remained on the stations. They came to live at Fitzroy Crossing, which, by the mid-1970s, had swelled to a major refugee town of over two thousand people. The vast majority of these people were Walmajarri, Wangkajunga, Gooniyandi and Nyikina, who suffered the same fate as the Bunuba in the wake of the pastoral industry restructure. The Bunuba, who numbered fewer than three hundred people, became a minority in their own country.

The Aboriginal population of Fitzroy Crossing declined rapidly in the 1980s, owing to the purchase of several pastoral properties by the Federal Government, on behalf of Aboriginal communities. As well, a number of small homeland communities were established through the policy of the State Government in the mid-1980s, which encouraged the excising of tiny living areas of land from pastoral leases.

Throughout this period the Bunuba remained landlocked in Fitzroy Crossing, denied access to their country by the pastoralists, who also refused to surrender any part of their leases for living areas.

It was not just the pastoralists who expropriated Bunuba land. In the 1960s the State Government turned Bandilngan (Windjana Gorge), Baraa (Tunnel Creek) and Danggu (Geikie Gorge) into national parks. The Bunuba were locked out of their most treasured places as thousands of tourists enjoyed the splendour of these sites, without knowing much about the violent battles fought a century earlier on this very land.

In 1992 and 1995, less than one hundred years after Jandamarra's death, the Bunuba took back Leopold Downs and Fairfield stations, following their purchase with Federal funding. The country was handed back with little fanfare or public recognition that hundreds of Bunuba had died in its defence only a few generations earlier. That was the way the Bunuba wanted it – to return quietly and fulfil a dream that Jandamarra and others had fought and died for: the opportunity to live independently from whites and to practice their law and traditions.

The Bunuba renamed these stations Yaranggi and Yuwa, and see them as a basis of social renewal, while still running them as cattle stations. For the first time in nearly forty years young boys now go through ceremonies of induction to Bunuba law in the country of Jandamarra. Life and culture have returned to the land.

Only months after the Bunuba took back possession of Yaranggi, the High Court, in *Mabo and Others v the State of Queensland*, by a majority of six to one, ruled that a form of Indigenous or Native Title existed for the Meriam, traditional owners of Mer, Dauar and Waier Islands in the Torres Strait, and had always existed at common law since the time of first settlement in 1788. The insidious doctrine of Terra Nullius – the legal fiction that Australia was unpeopled prior to white occupation or inhabited by people with no recognised social or political organisation – was assigned to the scrapheap of history.

Within months of the historic Native Title decision, several hundred Aboriginal people from throughout the Kimberley met at Wamali on Leopold Downs to talk about what the decision meant. This was the first Indigenous response to the High Court's recognition of their inherent legal rights and it took place within sight of where Jandamarra died. In welcoming the participants of the meeting, the Bunuba hosts spoke of this coincidence of history. This meeting led to Kimberley Aboriginal people being at the forefront of the debate that soon after engulfed Australian politics.

In making their Native Title judgement, Justices Gaudron and Deane said, 'The acts and events by which that dispossession in legal theory was carried into practical effect constitute the darkest aspect of the history of this nation. The nation as a whole must remain diminished unless and until there is an acknowledgment of, and retreat from, those injustices.'

In December 1992, the Prime Minister of Australia, Paul Keating, in a major speech to launch the International Year of the World's Indigenous Peoples, acknowledged on behalf of white Australia the past crimes and injustices inflicted on Aboriginal people:

> It was we who did the dispossessing. We took the traditional lands and smashed the traditional way of life; we brought the diseases, the alcohol; we committed the murders; we took the children from their mothers; we practised discrimination and exclusion. It was our ignorance and our prejudice, and our failure to imagine these things being done to us. With some noble exceptions, we failed to make the most basic human response and enter into their hearts and minds. We failed to ask: 'How would I feel if this were done to me?' As a consequence, we failed to see that what we were doing degraded all of us . . . Imagine if ours was the oldest culture in the world and that we were told that it was worthless . . . Imagine if we had suffered the injustice and then were blamed for it . . . Gradually we are learning how to see Australia through Aboriginal eyes, beginning to recognise the wisdom in their epic story.

The saga of Jandamarra and the Bunuba resistance is an epic story among many epic stories. This book is just one contribution to a greater understanding and appreciation of the horrors experienced, on the Australian frontier, by those whose lands were being invaded.

There are many Jandamarras who figure in the grim recital of Australia's colonisation. Their stories exist in the living memories of Aboriginal people and in the historical archives of our public libraries. Their telling should not elicit guilt but rather enrich our collective understanding of the suffering experienced by Aboriginal people from being dispossessed of their lands. It is an experience that cannot be quarantined to the past. The violence on the frontier between whites and the traditional owners has left an enduring legacy. It has largely determined the economic and social condition of Aboriginal communities over generations and continues to haunt the conscience of white Australia.

The tragedy of the Jandamarra story is that the colonisers were not prepared to negotiate with the traditional owners. They fought for total victory, demanding permanent Aboriginal subjugation. The Western Australian Government has been reluctant to recognise the rights that Aboriginal people died for, or were imprisoned en masse defending, not so long ago.

The Bunuba people are still seeking ownership and management of most of their country. Some of the pastoralists whose leases occupy Bunuba land continue to deny the traditional owners access to their country. The Bunuba are locked out of any real management of the lands they know better than anybody else. Bandilngan (Windjana Gorge), Baraa (Tunnel Creek), Danggu (Geikie Gorge) and a new national park that takes in much of Ganimbiri (Oscar Range) are state-owned and run by public servants who live in Perth. Efforts by the Bunuba to negotiate a major role in management for the traditional owners have been strenuously resisted by the State Government.

The Bunuba are still waiting for non-Aboriginal people to negotiate with them on the use of their country. Until there is that negotiated settlement between traditional owners and non-Aboriginal people, who continue to benefit from the original invasion and dispossession, past grievances will remain unresolved and a shared future will be impossible to plan. The legacy of Jandamarra is the challenge for this nation to achieve the coexistence of Indigenous peoples and those who have come to live on Aboriginal land.

PIGEON STORY

THE FOLLOWING IS FROM AN interview that Banjo Woorunmurra did with *Stephen Muecke in 1985. Banjo refers to Jandamarra as Pigeon, reflecting the popular understanding of the time.*

Now
PIGEON
Pigeon Start OFF, him bin –
I talk to you with the Pidgin English,
Pidgin – white man tongue, Pidgin –
he bin start off
breakin in HORSES
him bin SHEARER
shearin sheep with a BLADE
not a machine
'cos those days they had a blade,
so he bin work on that one, shearin blade
he bin work Quanbun Noonkanbah Liveringa
then he went back to Kimberley Down
he work there

an he went back to p'lice camp
then he start p'trol
he went for p'trol, look around some BLACKFELLAS inna bush
he tracking
(long pause)
What they done?
they killed two white man in Mount Broome
then p'lice went up to find him
so they pick-im-up – Pigeon the outlaw
they take-im in up on the range
then Pigeon walk up, an he got a MOB
an he bring them back
SOME was there
right one that bin kill the white man
but he didn't know who he was –
take him to Windjana Gorge tie them there
they turn around tell 'im Pigeon
'Alright you wanna get a kangaroo . . . for us?'
'We can't jus sitting down here stave hungry on the chain'
'You bin bring us'
'So you mus FEED us' –
SO –
Pigeon turn around and see boss, the boss –
'I wanna get a kangaroo for these prisoners'
'Alright you know where the rifle'
so he went up and get the rifle
'stead of he go for KANGAROO he shot his boss
in Windjana
Lillimooloora
that was a p'lice station –
(softly) Anyhow

he went there
got the mob
take-im off the chain an he bin go in the hill
everyone followed him up there
but he the one done all the FIGHTING
an this OTHERS didn't understand him
(softly) they never have-im fight –
Anyhow he went across to Ninety-Two
he shot one white man there
then he went to Oscar
Oscar Range station
he shot one white man there
early morning
then he went down to Plum Plain
he see MOB comin-up, gotta horse
stockboys and the p'liceman they ALL come look for Pigeon
then he take off from that big plain
Plum Plain
they chased him –
when he got into the HILL country
he look back
he knock that hats off the p'liceman
take his hat off –
(knocks table) one bullet
he asks that p'liceman he says
'You want you life or wanta dead'
p'liceman said 'No I wanta life'
'You get back'
so he just tease-im but if he wanted-im he hadda kill-im then
anyhow he let-im go
he went to Brooking Gorge, corner of Brooking or Leopold

an' he went toooo –
(long pause)
he went to King Leopold
an' he went tooo
he get a mob of blackfella there, big tribe
they start fight there –
they take-it away one woman from there, young girl
they couldn't fight-im
they couldn't foller-im
went back to Windjana
he bin fight for SIX YEARS and ah –
governor or government went up there and said
he went up he get up he's there Pigeon 'You there?' – 'Yes' –
'I'm here' –
Ah –
'Well we all friend now you'll have to come down' –
so Pigeon didn't take a risk
so he knock his hat said 'You better go off' –
said 'Ah I don't want to . . .'
knock his hat off this government bloke whatever he was
anyhow he went back agin
so [laugh]
stay there too long –
anyhow they follered-im up – so LAS he felt himself
he was . . . he was losing hope
they can put a bullet right across here
shootin-im in here
nothing can come out
not even water
not even a drop of blood
(softly) nothin doin

no matter how many shot he used to take her nothing doin
THAT didn't put him back
anyhow one mabarn blackfella witchdoctor –
come from ROEBOURNE –
they used to call-im ah Minko Mick* –
he got onto the boat in Roebourne
or Onslow
boat call – er . . . name . . . ah
Koombana, three funnel
come right up to Derby landed –
anyhow blackfella got onto mail coaches
they take-im to Meda and from Meda to Kimberley Downs
and from Kimberley Downs to Fairfield
then he ride across with horse
horseback
went to Tunnel
he SLEEP one night there
he didn't go fast
but next morning they stirred-im Pigeon up
so he got up to start shooting –
but this bloke seen his life
soo – witchdoctor told them boys
'Alright'
'I know' he said
'I take jus one bullet in my rifle' he said
'I'll kill-im an you fellas can go . . . cut his HEAD off'
so this Pigeon went up . . . aaah –
Minko Mick followed the river up
he got into the boab tree
he look up upwards
Pigeon was right on top in the cliff –

so he FIRE ONE shot he knock him in his thumb –
so he fell down, an he sing out
'I shoot-im you can go in and pick-im up whenever you want'
very fright they said, 'NO we can't run up to pick-im up'
'NO – you go in an see-im'
'He's finished'
'Alright'
oh well they didn't argue with im all them fellas round up there
and see –
sure enough Pigeon laying there
smashed up 'is thumb
so when Minko Mick – went up there he looked 'is thumb
he found a little
little heart like a fish
in his thumb here (shows thumb)
that where he shot an he pick-im-up
cut his HEAD off
an that was the end of the old Pigeon story –

it's from Banjo
Pandanus Park

*Contrary to official archives Minko Mick and Roebourne Micki are portrayed
as the same person in the Jandamarra oral history.

KIMBERLEY LANGUAGE GROUPS

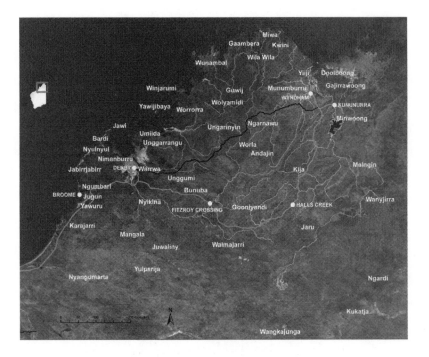

MAPS OF THE KIMBERLEY

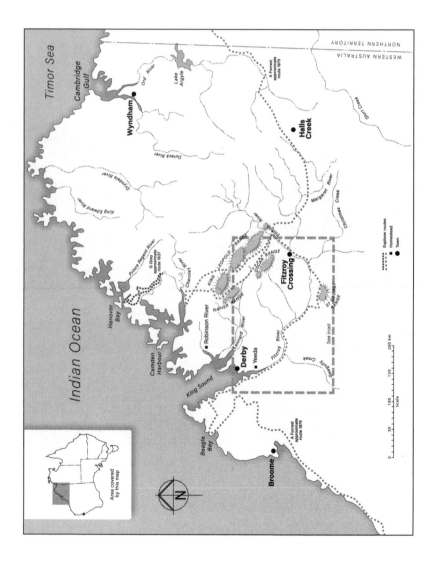

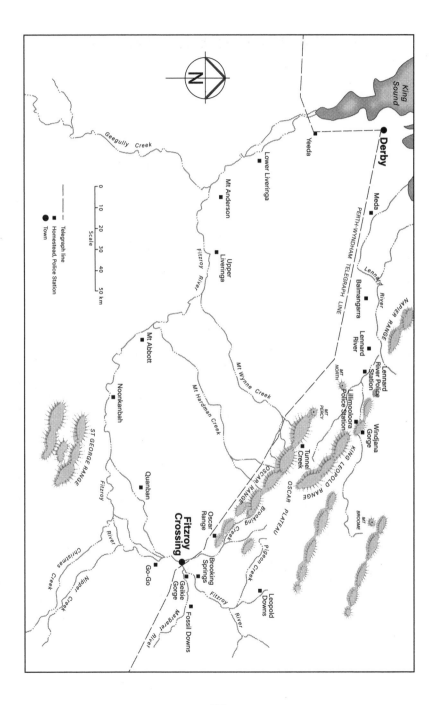

NOTES

CSO = Colonial Secretary's Office

COLONISATION

1. House of Commons Report quoted in Reynolds, H. *The Law of the Land*, Penguin, Melbourne, 1987, p85
2. Milne, J. *The Romance of a Pro Counsel*, London, 1911, p15
3. *Expeditions in Western Australia*, Sir George Grey papers, 1837–1839
4. The *Inquirer*, Perth, 20 July 1865
5. *ibid*, 3 December 1879
6. CSO, 16 December 1883 letter from J. McLarty to WC Marmion, 1530/1–1883
7. Despatches from Governor Broome to Secretary of State for the Colonies, Despatch no. 64, 21 August 1883, Reel 1696
8. The *Morning Herald*, Fremantle, 28 October 1882
9. The *West Australian*, Perth, 1 July 1884
10. CSO, 30 April 1885, 1612/85
11. *ibid*

CONFLICT

1. CSO, September 1886, 3922/86
2. *ibid*
3. CSO, 3377/86
4. Police Department, Derby Police Occurrence Book, 12 August 1886
5. CSO, letter from Isadore Emanuel to Colonial Secretary, 1496/88
6. The *Western Mail*, Perth, 28 March 1889
7. The *West Australian*, Perth, 21 November 1888
8. The *Western Mail*, Perth, 2 March 1889
9. *ibid*
10. The *Western Mail*, Perth, 23 March 1889
11. The *West Australian*, Perth, 11 August 1889
12. Votes and Proceedings, Legislative Council Address number 16, 1888
13. CSO, 16 May 1888 Police report, 1496/88
14. CSO, 3398/89
15. The *Western Mail*, Perth, 30 November 1889
16. *ibid*, 7 December 1889
17. *ibid*

THE LAND BETWEEN

1. The *Western Mail*, Perth, 29 October 1892
2. CSO, Perth, 20 September 1889 letter to Police Commissioner, 2909/89
3. The *West Australian*, Perth, 16 June 1892
4. The *North West Times*, Roebourne, 9 July 1892
5. CSO, July 1892 PC Armitage Report, 939/92
6. Police Department, Derby Letterbook, 1893
7. Gunning, EA *Diary of a Linesman*, Telegraph Station, Perth, 19 June 1894, unpublished

STATE OF SIEGE

1. The *West Australian*, Perth, 25 November 1893
2. Truthful Thomas, *Through the Looking Glass*, January 1905
3. The *West Australian*, Perth, 24 March 1894
4. The *West Australian*, Perth, 12 February 1894
5. *ibid*
6. Western Australian Parliamentary Debates, 1893, pp1051–1052
7. *ibid*
8. *ibid*
9. *ibid*, p241
10. The *North West Times*, Roebourne, 10 February 1894
11. *ibid*, 28 July 1894

REBELLION

1. *Catholic Record*, Perth,10 August 1893
2. CSO, Perth, from Sub-inspector Drewry Report to Commissioner Phillips 1893
3. Police Department, Derby Police Letter-book, Volume 22 1893, Sub-inspector Drewry to PC Clifton, 21 July 1893
4. *ibid*, from Sub-inspector Drewry to Commissioner Phillips, 10 March 1894
5. *ibid*, from Sub-inspector Drewry to Commissioner Phillips, 28 July 1894
6. *ibid*, telegram from Commissioner Phillips to Sub-inspector Drewry
7. *ibid*
8. Pilmer, RH *Men's Work – An Australian Saga*, 1937, p15, unpublished
9. *ibid*, p17
10. *ibid*, p33
11. Police Department, 15 December 1894, Sub-inspector Drewry Report, 3548/97

EXTREME MEASURES

1. Police Department, Perth,12 November 1894, Telegram from J. Forrest to RM Warton and W. Lukin, 3548/97
2. The *Western Mail*, Perth, 8 December 1894
3. Western Australian Parliamentary Debates, Volume 7, Perth, 1894, p1357
4. Police Department, Perth, 10 November 1894, Telegram from Commissioner Phillips to Sub-inspector Drewry, 3548/97
5. *ibid*
6. *ibid*
7. *ibid*
8. Western Australian Parliamentary Debates, Volume 7, Perth, 1894, p1357
9. *ibid*
10. The *West Australian*, Perth, 16 November 1894
11. The *Daily News*, Perth, 14 November 1894
12. Police Department, Perth, 23 January 1895, Sub-inspector Drewry Report, 3548/97
13. *ibid*, 19 November 1894, Telegram from Sub-inspector Drewry to Commissioner Phillips
14. *ibid*, 22 November 1894, Telegram from Commissioner Phillips to Lawrence
15. *ibid*, 16 December 1894
16. *ibid*, 28 December 1894, Telegram from Lawrence to Commissioner Phillips
17. *ibid*, Lawrence Diary, 27 December 1894

18. *ibid*, 29 December 1894, Telegram from Commissioner Phillips to Lawrence
19. Hawke, S. and Gallagher, M. *Noonkanbah*, Fremantle Arts Centre Press, Fremantle, 1989, p50
20. Police Department, Perth 10 March 1895, Lawrence Diary, 3548/97
21. The *Northern Public Opinion*, Roebourne, 2 February 1895

RESURRECTION
1. Police Department, Perth, 10 December 1894, Telegram from RM Warton to Premier Forrest, 3548/97
2. The *Western Mail*, 22 December 1894
3. *ibid*
4. *Catholic Record*, 10 January 1895
5. *ibid*
6. CSO, 17 July 1895, Minute from Octavius Burt to Premier Forrest, 823/895
7. Western Australian Parliamentary Debates, 1896
8. Department of Aboriginal Affairs, 24 October 1896, Marsden Report, 2146/96
9. Police Department, January 1895, Letter from W. Lukin to Premier Forrest, 3548/97
10. CSO, 1 April 1895, Telegram from Commissioner Phillips to Sub-inspector Drewry, 893/95
11. *ibid*
12. *ibid*
13. Police Department, Derby Letterbook, 1895
14. *ibid*, 21 April 1895, Telegram to Commissioner Phillips
15. CSO, 3 May 1895, Telegram from Commissioner Phillips to Sub-inspector Drewry, 893/95
16. Police Department, Derby Letterbook, 27 July 1895, Telegram from PC Pilmer to Sgt Cadden
17. *ibid*, 31 July 1895, Telegram from Commissioner Phillips to Sgt Cadden

THE SPIRIT OF JANDAMARRA
1. Banjo Woorunmurra, as told to Howard Pedersen
2. Police Department, Perth, 29 February 1896, Telegram from Sub-inspector Ord to Commissioner Phillips, 653/96
3. *ibid*
4. *ibid*, Sub-inspector Ord Report, March 1896
5. Western Australian Parliamentary Debates, 1896

FIGHT TO THE END
1. The *Northern Public Opinion*, Roebourne, 13 February 1897
2. *ibid*, 5 June 1897
3. *ibid*
4. The *Northern Public Opinion*, Roebourne, 23 July 1897
5. Police Department, Perth, 5 May 1897, Sub-inspector Ord Report, 3548/97
6. *ibid*, 18 March 1897, Ord Journal, 9/41897
7. The *T'othersider*, Kalgoorlie, March 1897
8. Police Department, 18 March to 9 April 1897, Ord Journal, 3548/97
9. *ibid*, 27 March 1897, PC Chisholm Journal
10. *ibid*

BIBLIOGRAPHY

1. Published Primary Sources
   a. Official Documents
   (i)

Western Australian Parliamentary Papers Votes and Proceedings of Legislative Council,
   1880–97

   (ii)   Western Australian Parliamentary Debates, 1881–94
   (iii)   Western Australian Bluebooks, 1880–97
   (iv)   Western Australian Statutes, 1886–92

   b. Newspapers
   (i)   The *Daily News*, Perth
   (ii)   The *Inquirer*, Perth
   (iii)   The *Morning Herald*, Fremantle
   (iv)   The *North West Times*, Roebourne
   (v)   The *Northern Public Opinion*, Roebourne
   (vi)   The *Pilbara Goldfield Times*, Roebourne
   (vii)   The *T'othersider*, Kalgoorlie
   (viii)   The *West Australian*, Perth
   (ix)   The *Western Mail*, Perth

2. Unpublished Primary Sources
   (i)   Files of the Colonial Secretary's Office, 1883–96
   (ii)   Files of the Police Department, 1886–97
   (iii)   Supreme Court Records, 1892, Supreme Court, WA
   (iv)   Secretary of State Despatches to the Governor, 1885–87

3. Secondary Sources

Anderson, L *The Role of Aboriginal and Asian Labour in the Origin and Development of the Early Pearling Industry, Broome, WA*, BA (Hons) Thesis, Murdoch University, 1978, unpublished

Balfour, H *On the Methods Employed in the Manufacture of Glass Spearheads*, Man. Vol. 3, 1905

Biskup, P *Not Slaves, Not Citizens*, University of Queensland Press, St Lucia, 1975

Buchanan, G *Packhorse and Waterhole: With the First Overlanders to the Kimberley*, Sydney, 1935

Cannon, M *The Land Boomers*, Melbourne University Press, Melbourne, 1978

Christie, MF *Aborigines in Colonial Victoria 1835–86*, Sydney University Press, Sydney

Crowley, FK *John Forrest 1847–1918*, Volume One, 1847–91 Apprenticeship to Premiership, University of Queensland Press, St Lucia, 1971

Durack, M 'The Outlaws to Windjinah Gorge', *Walkabout*, June, 1941

Elkin, AP 'Native Reaction to an Invading Culture and its Bearers, with Special Reference to Australia', Proceedings of the 7th Pacific Science Congress, Christchurch, 1953

Elkin, AP 'Reaction and Interaction', *American Anthropologist*, Vol. 53, 1951

Elkin, AP 'Social Organisation in the Kimberley Division', *Oceania*, Vol. 2, 1931–32

Fannon, F *Black Skin White Masks*, Paladin, St Albans, 1973

Flinders, CE 'North West Memoirs', The *Western Mail*, 2 January 1947

Froggett, WW *Accounts of Travels of the Kimberley*, unpublished manuscript held in Mitchell Library, Sydney, 1887

Gill, A 'Aborigines, Settlers and Police in the Kimberley 1887–1905', Studies in Western
    Australian History, University of Western Australia, Perth 1977
Gribble, JB Dark Deeds in a Sunny Land, The Daily News, Perth, 1905
Halls, C Guns of Australia, Sydney, 1914
Hasluck, P Black Australians: A Survey of Native Policy in Western Australia, 1829–1897,
    Melbourne University Press, Melbourne, 1942, 2nd Edition, 1970
Haydon, AL The Trooper Police of Australia, London, 1911
Hobsbawn, EJ Primitive Rebels: Study in archaic forms of social movement in the nineteenth and
    twentieth centuries, Manchester, 1963
Hunt, SJ The Gribble Affair: A Study of Aboriginal-European Labour Relations in North-West
    Australia during the 1880s, BA (Hons) Thesis, Murdoch University, 1978, unpublished
Idriess, IL Outlaws of the Leopolds, Angus and Robertson, Sydney, 1952
ibid Over the Range: Sunshine and Shadow in the Kimberleys, Angus and Robertson, Sydney,
    1951
Marchant, L 'Native Administration in Western Australia', BA (Hons) Thesis, University of
    Western Australia, 1954, unpublished
McQuilton, J The Kelly Outbreak 1878–1880: The Geographical Dimension of Social Banditry,
    Melbourne University Press, Melbourne, 1979
Memmi, A The Colonizer and the Colonized, Souvenir Press, London, 1974
Pilmer, RH 'Northern Patrol (Compiled from the Diaries of RH Pilmer by CH Christie)',
    Countryman, 30 August, and 6, 13, 20, and 27 September 1956
Reece, R Aborigines and Colonists, Sydney University Press, Sydney, 1974
Reynolds, H Aborigines and Settlers: The Australian Experience 1788–1939, Cassell, Melbourne,
    1972
Rowley, CD The Destruction of Aboriginal Society, ANU Press, Canberra, 1970
Stannage, CT 'The Composition of the Western Australian Parliament 1890–1911', University
    Studies in History, Vol IV, No 4, 1966
Tindale, NB 'Distribution of Australian Aboriginal Tribes: A Field Study', Transactions of the
    Royal Society of South Australia, 1940

Ward, R The Australian Legend, Oxford University Press, Melbourne, 1958

ACKNOWLEDGEMENTS

THANK YOU TO EVERYONE WHO assisted me in the researching and writing of this book. I am indebted to the Bunuba people who trusted me with their history, a number of whom have now passed away. I will always be grateful to the old man from Derby, the last full Unggumi speaker, who died in 1993.

Aside from Banjo Woorunmurra, the custodian of the Jandamarra story, friends and family gave up their time to help me in ways too numerous to mention. Friends in the Kimberley and beyond helped sharpen my analysis and perspective over countless hours of conversation.

And thank you to Peter Bibby and Sandra Phillips whose skillful editing brought the manuscript to a point where I was happy for its release.

Howard Pedersen

PHOTO CREDITS

INDEX

This is a 🐾 Magabala Book

LEADING PUBLISHER OF ABORIGINAL AND
TORRES STRAIT ISLANDER STORYTELLERS.

CHANGING THE WORLD, ONE STORY AT A TIME.

First published 1995. Reprinted 2000, 2007.
New edition 2011. Reprinted 2012. Revised edition 2016, reprinted 2017, 2018, 2019 x2, 2021, 2023.
Magabala Books Aboriginal Corporation
1 Bagot Street, Broome, Western Australia
Website: www.magabala.com

Magabala Books receives financial assistance from the Commonwealth Government through the
Australia Council, its arts advisory body. The State of Western Australia has made an investment in this
project through the Department of Local Government, Sport and Cultural Industries. Magabala Books
would like to acknowledge the generous support of the Shire of Broome, Western Australia.

Magabala Books is Australia's only independent Aboriginal and Torres Strait Islander publishing house.
Magabala Books acknowledges the Traditional Owners of the Country on which we live and work. We
recognise the unbroken connection to traditional lands, waters and cultures. Through what we publish,
we honour all our Elders, peoples and stories, past, present and future.

Premier's Prize WA Premier's Book Awards 1996
Shortlisted NSW Premier's Literary Awards 1996

Cover Design Jo Hunt
Typeset by Post Pre-press Group
Printed and bound by Griffin Press, South Australia
Cover photograph Nigel Gaunt. Kimberley Maps Brenda Thorley.

A catalogue record for this book is available from the National Library of Australia

ISBN (Print) 978-1-925936-54-4

Aboriginal and Torres Strait Islander people are advised that this publication contains the names and
photographs of deceased persons. Where possible, approval has been obtained from the appropriate
people to publish these names and images.

This publication adopts the Kimberley Language Resource Centre (KLRC) standard and Magabala
Books expresses appreciation for their consultancy. The use of miles has been adopted to reflect the
historical setting.

Magabala Books acknowledges University of Queensland Press and Stephen Muecke for use of the
Pigeon Story